Scroll Saw
Puzzle
Patterns

Scroll Saw Puzzle Patterns

Patrick &
Patricia Spielman

 Sterling Publishing Co., Inc.   New York

Edited by Laurel Ornitz

Library of Congress Cataloging-in-Publication Data

Spielman, Patrick E.
   Scroll saw puzzle patterns / Patrick & Patricia Spielman.
      p.   cm.
   Includes index.
   ISBN 0-8069-6586-X (pbk.)
   1. Wooden toy making. 2. Puzzles. I. Spielman, Patricia.
II. Title.
TT174.5.W6S65 1988
688.7'26—dc19   88-19968
                                                            CIP

                         7 9 10

Copyright © 1988 by Patrick and Patricia Spielman
Published by Sterling Publishing Co., Inc.
387 Park Avenue South, New York, N.Y. 10016
Distributed in Canada by Sterling Publishing
% Canadian Manda Group, P.O. Box 920, Station U
Toronto, Ontario, Canada M8Z 5P9
Distributed in Great Britain and Europe by Cassell PLC
Artillery House, Artillery Row, London SW1P 1RT, England
Distributed in Australia by Capricorn Ltd.
P.O. Box 665, Lane Cove, NSW 2066
Manufactured in the United States of America
All rights reserved

Contents

INTRODUCTION *6*

1 Wood Materials *13*

2 Designing Wood Puzzles *23*

3 Basic Tools—Techniques and Tips *34*

4 Making Wooden Jigsaw Puzzles *61*

Color section follows page 64.

5 Making Stand-Up Puzzles *68*

6 Making Inlay Puzzles *119*

7 Some Tricky Ideas *218*

8 Finishing and Painting Techniques *230*

METRIC EQUIVALENCY CHART *249*

ABOUT THE AUTHORS *250*

CURRENT BOOKS BY PATRICK SPIELMAN *251*

INDEX *254*

Introduction

Those familiar jigsaw puzzles that are mass-produced from slick cardboard are, perhaps, the best known and oldest type of puzzle. Jigsawing machines, or scroll saws, do not actually touch any part of the puzzle during the course of its production. Jigsaw puzzles, however, do derive their name from the jigsaws (scroll-cutting saws) that are used to make the dies that in turn cut the cardboard puzzle pieces.

The original pieces of the production puzzle are cut out of select, thick hardwood. These pieces are then supported by and locked together with thin metal dies that are raised above the wood so that their sharp edges can stamp out complete puzzles in one motion, or operation. Essentially, this technique remains the only practical method for producing puzzles in large numbers.

The earliest puzzles were individually cut by hand with fretsaws. An Englishman named John Spillsbury is credited with the invention of the jigsaw puzzle in 1760. Spillsbury applied hand-colored maps to thin sheets of mahogany, which he then cut along the various boundary lines. Spillsbury's puzzles were very expensive and marketed as "dissected maps for the teaching of geography."

The first die-cut jigsaw puzzles of cardboard were produced in the United States

Illus. 1. Scroll-sawn jigsaw puzzles for any age level are great fun and very easy to make.

Illus. 2. Two postcard jigsaw puzzles—one with six pieces, the other with 28.

during the early to mid-1800s. The term "dissected puzzles" evolved to "jigsaw puzzles," and puzzle making became a production business. Some of the early manufacturers listed "par times" for the assembly of their puzzles, and some individuals gained notoriety for their speed of puzzle completion. During the Depression years, puzzle clubs and contests flourished. Some famous American families—including the Rockefellers, Vanderbilts, and DuPonts—are known to have collected and played puzzles with intensity.

Other countries continued to make puzzles out of wood well into the late nineteenth century. In around 1914 plywood came into use; and for puzzle making, it is probably still the choice material of woodcrafters who cut their own jigsaw puzzles with modern scroll saws.

Today there is one well-known company in Suffolk, England, that still produces custom-made wooden jigsaw puzzles for worldwide markets by mail order. The customer provides a photograph or picture, and specifies the level of difficulty, which determines how the puzzle is to be cut.

These puzzles are made with a 4-mm 3-ply birch backing material.

If you own a scroll saw and employ just a few elementary techniques, you can produce your own custom-made jigsaw puzzles. See Illus. 1 and 2. Any picture, photo, map, postcard, or poster can be pasted on wood and then cut up into pieces to create a puzzle. The possibilities for making adult and children's jigsaw puzzles with your scroll saw are endless. Making these puzzles requires very little skill or imagination, and zero artistic talent. And, you can make them without much technical assistance.

However, as popular as jigsaw puzzles are, they are only a small part of this book because they're so easy to make on your own. The major thrust of this book deals with patterns and techniques for making two other types of children's wooden puzzles—the stand-up (Illus. 3) and the insert (Illus. 4 and 5). Insert puzzles are also called inlay, or tray, puzzles.

There is a growing interest in quality hand-crafted wooden children's puzzles, probably because they are easy to make;

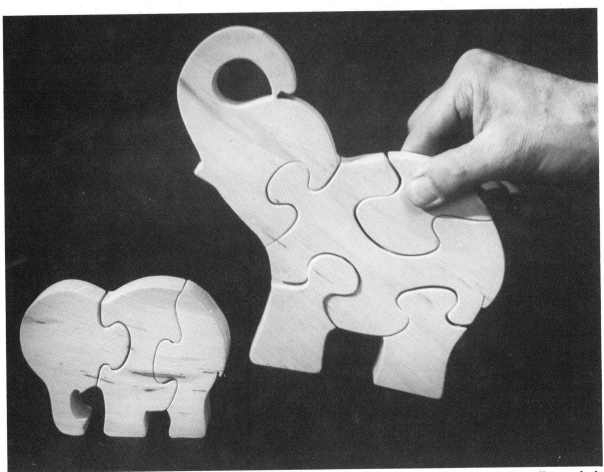

Illus. 3. Well-designed stand-up puzzles can be moved intact, as shown. Thick material, well-rounded edges, and smooth surfaces are other good characteristics. On the elephant on the right, note that the upper trunk is cut so that it remains connected to the head for strength.

children love them; parents love them for many reasons, but primarily for their great educational value; and they are big sellers at flea markets, gift and crafts shops, art shows, and bazaars. However, hand-made wooden stand-up and insert puzzles have a broader appeal to the general public than hand-made wooden jigsaw puzzles. This is because jigsaw puzzles tend to be more individualized to a specific person or customized to a particular subject.

To make stand-up and insert puzzles that are above the ordinary requires, first of all, high-quality, artistically designed patterns. Secondly, it's essential to make

innovative use of bright and vibrant colors that will captivate the minds and imaginations of the young puzzle users. Therefore, we have given these two basic requirements top priority in this book. You will find approximately 80 full-size patterns, and most of the significant puzzles are shown in full color. Consequently, you can copy the puzzles in every exact detail, right down to the precise shade and hue of a particular color.

Some of the traditional alphabet and number puzzles, along with the United States map, Raggy Ann, personalized air balloon (Illus. 5), and the clowns and rainbow designs are certain to be family classics. Some puzzles are so special that they can be hung on the wall of a child's room when not in use. Or, you can simply glue the pieces in permanently and use the puzzles solely for decoration.

In addition to providing full-size patterns, we have included helpful information about designing, selecting wood, and using a number of basic tool and machine techniques that will make your efforts easier and more efficient. We have also included tips on using stickers, decals, press type, and templates because they can add those special professional touches that don't require artistic talent but will still set your work well apart from others'.

And you'll find some easy-to-do but specific tips on painting details that can dramatically accentuate certain design features.

Should you want to turn your puzzle-making skills into a profitable enterprise, we have provided some new methods as well as a few traditional techniques for producing puzzles in quantities. Making puzzles is a good way for anyone, 10 years or older, to convert free time and energy into extra income. See Illus. 6 and 7.

However, puzzle making for the purpose of delighting and educating the youngsters in your family or neighborhood can be very rewarding in its own right—es-

Illus. 4. Puzzles of this type are called inlay, insert, or tray puzzles. They consist of two layers of thin-sheet wood material, usually plywood, that are glued together after the pieces of the upper layer have been cut free. The bottom piece is usually a lower grade of backing material.

pecially when you see those anxious little hands and minds manipulating your puzzle pieces to successful completion. Puzzle making is also enjoyable because you can make one or several from start to finish in a very short work period. Unlike furniture making, bird carving, or cabinet-making, puzzle making requires only a few skills, a minimum of time and tools, very little workshop space, and low-cost materials (Illus. 8 and 9). Whatever your purpose or intent in making wooden puzzles might be, we are sure you will find it to be a gratifying and fun woodcrafting experience.

Illus. 5. This popular air balloon puzzle can be personalized, as shown here.

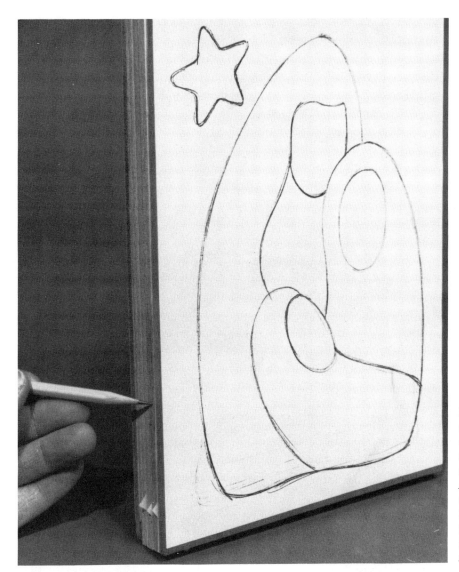

Illus. 6. Here's a job ready for production cutting. Five puzzles stacked together will all be cut at one time. A pattern produced on a photocopy machine has been temporarily bonded to the top layer to simplify and speed the layout.

Illus. 7. This is an example of production puzzle work accomplished by stack-cutting. With different wood species and selective staining, you can make five different varieties of basically identical puzzles.

Illus. 8. These puzzles are made of scrap framing materials from building construction.

Illus. 9. These 6″ × 6″ brain teasers are two-layer plywood puzzles. The little strips glued around the outside contain the puzzle pieces.

1

Wood Materials

There is a wide variety of wood material suitable for puzzle making. Some types of wood material are very common, readily available, and reasonably inexpensive. See Illus. 10. Other types are considered more extravagant; they are sometimes difficult to obtain and are always more expensive, but they're not essential to puzzle making. Great puzzles can be made from almost any type or grade of wood material. The outcome of a project usually has more to do with the design of the puzzle and the effort and overall craftsmanship put into it than with the choice of the raw material.

However, as you become more experienced in woodcrafting, you eventually will want to use materials that are appropriately matched to your skill level. No one expects a Chippendale effort to go into an ordinary 2 × 4.

Illus. 10. Typical 2 × 4 and 2 × 6 softwood construction timbers can be used for making some stand-up puzzles. Thicknesses are actually 1½".

The wood material used for making the majority of the puzzles in this book falls into two general categories: solid lumber and sheet material (plywoods and hardboard). We'll briefly discuss some of the advantages and disadvantages of both.

Solid Lumber

Solid woods are primarily used for making stand-up puzzles, as shown in Illus. 10 and 11. You can use either a softwood or a hardwood species, depending on your individual preference. However, in order to cut heavy or thick hardwoods effectively, you will need to use a high-quality scroll saw. The saw must have the capability of making consistently true, vertical cuts without any distortion or deflection of the cut surfaces, which could inhibit the interlocking functions of the puzzle pieces.

Typical softwood 2 × 4s or 2 × 6s and similar lumber used in building construction are ideal for certain stand-up puzzles.

You can often find good scraps of this material in quantities at building sites, and they are usually free for the asking. Of course, you can go to your local building supplier and buy lengths of new construction wood inexpensively. But do not use any pressure-treated varieties because this material may contain harmful preservatives.

Most construction lumber of any quality is kiln-dried, which is good because kiln-dried material has a good resistance against distortion and checking. It is usually labeled as a S-P-F species, which means that any piece pulled from the pile may be either spruce, pine, or fir. You might as well buy the lower grades of this material if there are not too many knots, twists, checks, waney edges, or other defects that would interfere with the puzzle work. If the wood has too many of these defects, the better grades might prove to be the economical advantage.

Today's 2 × 4s and 2 × 6s are actually

Illus. 11. Some good, solid wood species include, from left to right, white pine, sugar pine, hard maple, and soft maple.

just 1½″ thick and 3½″ and 5½″ in width, respectively. See Illus. 10. A good thickness for stand-up puzzles is 1½″. Puzzles that require a greater width than 5½″ can be made by gluing up stock edge to edge. See Illus. 12.

Another way to make wide and thick puzzle stock is to glue two wide boards that are ¾″ thick together face to face, as shown in Illus. 13. This creates an exceptionally good puzzle-making material because the built-up material has far less of a tendency to warp, distort, or crack than a single solid board of the same dimension.

Some lumber dealers and woodworking mail-order businesses will ship small quantities of wood to home and amateur woodworkers. Usually these sources sell the highest quality softwoods and some of the expensive exotics, as well. Poplar, white pine, sugar pine, soft maple, birch, and hard maple are all good choices. We especially like soft maple because it is a medium-density wood that cuts clean in

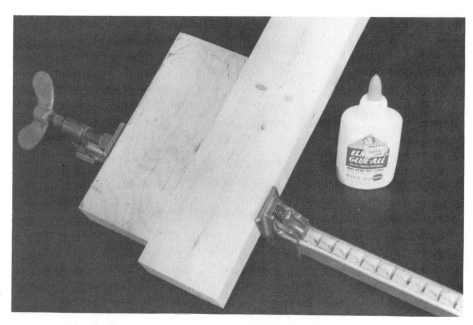

Illus. 12. You can make wider stock for stand-up puzzles by gluing 2 × 4s edge to edge. This minimizes warpage distortion and some of the internal stresses of large one-piece planks.

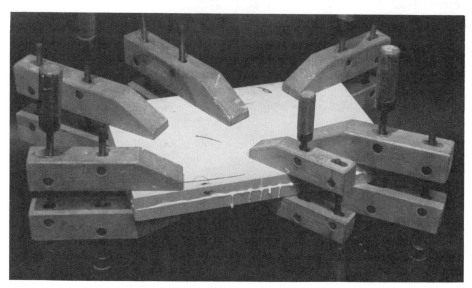

Illus. 13. Wide and thick stock—consisting of two or more layers of thinner boards glued up face to face, as shown— also makes ideal material. It has less tendency to split, crack, or warp than a single piece of wood of the same thickness.

thicker dimensions. It is neither too hard nor too soft. It is more abrasion-resistant than pine and just tougher overall. Soft maple finishes extremely well and takes inked line art perfectly, which is often necessary in creating small details—such as the eyes on animals.

Some softer woods—such as willow, pine, and butternut—are not practical if you anticipate that the puzzles will need to be able to withstand rougher than normal use. Certain children are more abusive to toys than others. When making puzzles for such children, you should also avoid the cedars, redwood, Douglas fir, and white fir because they generally tend to split and splinter more readily than other species.

Of course, if you know the temperament or maturity of the child, it's easier to make the appropriate selection of wood. We have used pine, the cedars, redwood, and butternut for certain custom-made functional and decorative puzzles. It is also important for the shape of the pieces to be of a certain configuration so that they will have minimal breaking tendencies. See Illus. 42 on page 35. You basically have to match the wood to the design of the puzzle and to the personality of the eventual user. Making puzzles for children you know is much less problematic than making puzzles to sell to the general public. When making puzzles to sell, we recommend using a medium-to-good grade of a quality species. Using the best materials, such as a solid hard maple or exotic veneer plywoods, will only drive the costs up. Incidentally, hard maple, oak, hickory, cherry, and similar heavy hardwoods will require an exceptional saw and good blades to be able to be cut effectively.

If you will be painting the wood with opaque finishes, then it's all right to use wood with various dents or knots. These defects can be filled, and will be hidden under the finish. But, if you intend to use transparent oils, stains, dyes, and the like, then a quality base wood material is the obvious and necessary choice.

Every woodworker should have a good local resource person from whom he can seek advice and assistance in obtaining the right material for his particular craft. It would be especially helpful if this person were your local building-products dealer who could show you samples and make suggestions from the line and grades of material that he sells.

Serious woodworkers should have their own machine for surfacing or planing solid wood boards, or have access to some place where this can be done. See Illus. 14.

Illus. 14. Board surfaces can be cleaned with sanders or made flat and true with a small home-shop planer, such as this. Here, thin stock is surfaced while supported on plywood. Both pieces are fed into the machine simultaneously.

Sheet Material

Sheet material essentially includes hardboards and plywoods. Plywoods can have either hardwood or softwood faces and

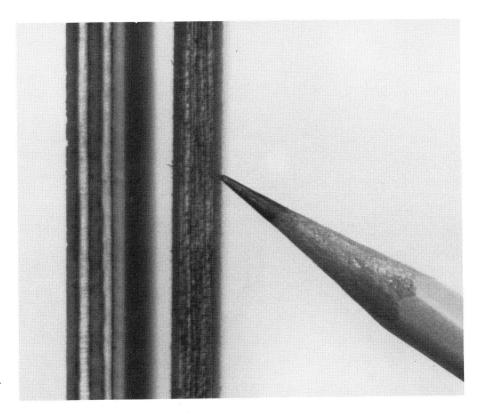

Illus. 15. The five-ply edge of Baltic birch plywood (on the left) being compared to typical three-ply hardwood plywood.

various kinds of material for the cores or inner plies. See Illus. 15.

Hardboard Hardboard (Illus. 16) is a remanufactured panel of hot-pressed wood fibres. Hardboard is generally less expensive than plywood. Since hardboard panels have no grain or pattern, they don't have any knots, checks, voids, or other de-

Illus. 16. Hardboard is used for jigsaw puzzles and as backing on cheaper insert, or tray, puzzles. Hardboard is available locally in ⅛″ and ¼″ thicknesses and in tempered and standard varieties. The tempered variety is tougher and more expensive.

fects that you might find in wood plywoods. However, hardboard is uninteresting and boring to look at.

Hardboard comes in two basic types: standard and tempered. Tempered is much stronger, stiffer, and smoother, and much more water-resistant than standard. Both types of hardboard are available in ⅛" and ¼" thicknesses. Hardboard can be used as an inexpensive backing for jigsaw and insert (inlay) puzzles. The tempered variety is always the better choice although it can't replace the look or feel of real wood. The standard variety would only be acceptable as a backing on inexpensive, low-quality insert puzzles. Hardboard tends to be a real pain to finish. It does not take stains or dyes well at all, and the application of satisfactory, brightly colored, opaque top coats requires a great deal of preparation.

Plywood Certain types of *softwood plywood* are generally not well suited to some kinds of puzzles. Douglas fir and southern pine plywoods are two readily available species, but they tend to splinter (Illus. 17 and 18) and are also somewhat abusive to saw blades. However, thin Douglas fir plywood (¼") can be used as backing layers on insert puzzles, provided appropriate precautions are taken. For instance, all sharp edges need to be thoroughly rounded and sanded, and the wood also needs to be well sealed and finished with at least two tough top coats. We feel that Douglas fir and southern pine plywoods only look good when covered

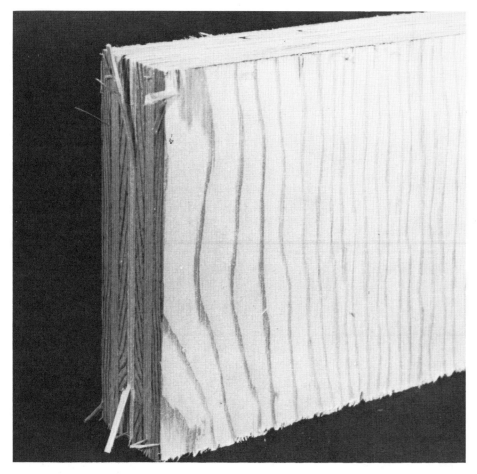

Illus. 17. This photo clearly shows the splintering tendencies of fir plywood. It is best avoided, and definitely not recommended for puzzles that may receive hard use. If used, be sure to round over all edges and seal thoroughly.

Illus. 18. Slivering, as shown here on this ¼" fir puzzle backing, is obviously very dangerous. Lower grades of Baltic birch will also sliver this way. Be certain to round over all edges and corners and to seal them well to minimize this serious condition.

with opaque finishes that completely conceal their natural colors and coarse grain patterns. One type of softwood plywood worth considering, if you can obtain it locally, is Douglas fir with a resin-impreg-nated kraft paper overlay on the face surfaces. See Illus. 19. Some plywoods also have abrasive resin adhesives that tend to dull blades quickly. See Illus. 20.

Lauan-faced plywood (Illus. 20 and 21) is

Illus. 19. Some heavy plywoods, from top to bottom: seven-ply ⅜" Baltic birch, 13-ply ¾" Baltic birch, seven-ply ¾" veneer-core domestic birch, nine-ply ¾" lauan exterior grade, five-ply ¾" fir with resin-coated paper overlay, and typical five-ply ¾" fir plywood.

19

a better all-around choice, but it is a very porous and absorbent material that really sucks up stain and paint. But it's usually very economical, and makes a good backing for insert puzzles.

Hardwood Plywood (Illus. 22) that is about ¼″ thick is an excellent choice for the top layers or the form piece of insert puzzles. The most popular species of hardwood plywood are domestic birch or the imported Baltic birch. See Illus. 21. Baltic birch is much stronger than domestic birch. It has more plies than conventional plywood, as you can see in Illus. 15, 21, and 23. "B" is the premium grade of Baltic birch, which compares roughly to an "A" grade in domestic plywood. "BB" and "CP" are other Baltic birch face grades available in a descending order of quality.

Domestic hardwood plywood grades

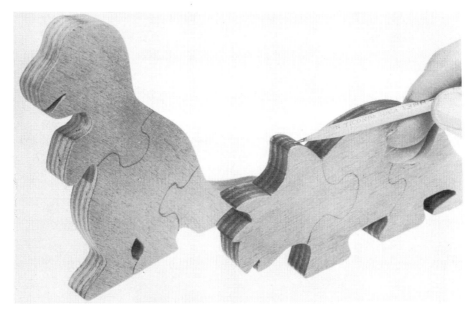

Illus. 20. The abrasive glue layers of this exterior lauan plywood has quickly dulled a new blade, as evidenced by the charred sawn surfaces on just this second puzzle cut-out.

Illus. 21. These are some of the less expensive plywoods. On the left, note the edges of typical ¼″-thick three-ply plywood compared to the five-ply edges of Baltic birch. The panels, from left to right, are ¼″ lauan, ¼″ fir, ¼″ Baltic birch, ¼″ domestic birch, and 4-mm (⁵⁄₃₂″) Baltic birch.

Illus. 22. A good choice for some puzzles is ¾″ veneer-core birch plywood. Note how clean and smooth the sawn, unsanded surfaces are.

Illus. 23. The design profile of this puzzle requires a very strong material, such as Baltic birch plywood. The tail, horns, and ears would be very fragile if sawn from solid wood.

range from premium (No. 1) downwards to "utility" and "backing" grades numbers 3 and 4, respectively. For inlay puzzles, only one face needs to be of a better grade.

Check with your building materials supplier for hardwood plywood. Incidentally, you may be able to get in touch with some good alternative sources through the Yellow Pages. Also, cabinet shops can often be a good source for small hardwood plywood cutoffs. Sometimes you can find exquisite material in suitable sizes at very attractive prices. See Illus. 24.

Illus. 24. Three-ply ¼″ veneer-hardwood plywoods, from left to right: walnut, birch, cherry, oak, and teak.

2

Designing Wood Puzzles

Sooner or later, for one reason or another, you may want to consider certain options that have to do with designing your own puzzles or making modifications to our patterns. Although we have included many ready-to-use patterns for what we think are very good designs, they can still be customized or modified to become even more personal and practical for a specific user.

For example, a puzzle may need to be changed if you want to alter the level of difficulty from the way it was originally designed. Increasing or decreasing the number of pieces and changing their shapes and sizes will have a definite effect on the level of difficulty.

Generally, jigsaw (scroll-saw) puzzles for 12 years and up are considered average in difficulty if their pieces are approximately ¾″ to 1″ square. Children's puzzles for ages 4 through 11 fall in the average range if their pieces are about 1¼″ to 1½″ square; larger pieces up to about 3″ square are suitable for ages 3 to 7. See Illus. 25 and 26.

Some other elements can be incorporated into the design of a puzzle to make it easier or more difficult to assemble. With insert puzzles, one very simple way to in-crease the difficulty level is to make the puzzle pieces double-sided. This is accomplished by painting both the top and underside surfaces of all the pieces. When making insert puzzles for younger children, it is therefore best to paint the upper, or face, surfaces only and leave the underside unpainted. Stand-up puzzles need to be finished on all surfaces for obvious aesthetic reasons. Pieces for stand-up puzzles can be separated or combined to increase or decrease the difficulty as desired.

An adult jigsaw puzzle can be made very challenging simply by cutting it into many small pieces and making all the pieces double-sided—that is, making the puzzle with a picture on both the top and bottom surfaces. If you want to make the puzzle extremely challenging and drive the puzzle assembler absolutely insane, make the puzzle with identical images on both sides (surfaces).

You need to be careful not to inadvertently design or build disturbing frustrations into a child's puzzle. The puzzle shown in Illus. 27 can serve as a good example. If the sawn frame surrounding the pieces was not cut perfectly, the puzzle

Illus. 25. If you need a pattern, this one can be enlarged or reduced on a copy machine to make puzzle pieces of the desired size.

pieces could only be assembled one way within the frame, that is, assembled only exactly the way all of the pieces were originally cut out. Should the child attempt to assemble the puzzle with the frame at a position that is inverted from the original way it was sawn out, he would probably become frustrated. Illus. 28 shows an improved design that is very similar but without the sawn frame surrounding the puzzle parts. The same design idea is carried to a higher level of difficulty in Illus. 29. This puzzle shows how you can incor-

porate additional pieces within a surrounding background and frame. However, this type of frame is less frustrating to match pieces to than the type of frame in Illus. 27.

When designing or modifying puzzles, always try to make shapes without sharp corners. Sharp corners on puzzles for toddlers can be dangerous. Also, corners can break off on pointed shapes, and very narrow pieces of short-grained solid wood can snap easily. Illus. 30 shows two types of interlocking puzzle pieces. One is a good design in that it has all rounded corners; the other is much less desirable because it has sharp, fragile corners.

If your designs have parts that appear to be fragile, then it's best to use plywood. Baltic birch plywood is, for the most part, equally tough in all directions to the face grain. However, you should be aware that thick or built-up layers of some plywoods are very difficult to saw accurately. Incidentally, stand-up puzzles sawn from thick wood have a better and more stable look than the same design cut from a thinner material. See Illus. 31.

Personalizing a puzzle is a simple design technique that can make a good puzzle even more special. Painting on a name, cutting certain puzzle parts in specific shapes, and painting the puzzle in an individual's favorite colors are easy ways to personalize a puzzle. Certain personalization techniques require some artistic tal-

ent, but the various items discussed below are available to help.

Templates (Illus. 32) are available at arts and crafts shops, and they are helpful in creating letters and numbers for subsequent woodburning or hand painting. Rub-on, or transfer, lettering, also available at most arts and crafts shops, is easy to use; however, be sure to finish (seal) the surfaces first and to apply adequate protective top coats over the applied letters. See Illus. 33 and 34.

Don't overlook the use of water-transferred decals. They are self-adhesive and waterproof once applied to wood. Application is very easy, but the raw wood surfaces must first be well sealed and finished. All sorts of imaginative designs are available in decal art—such as alphabets, numbers, birds, teddy bears, and favorite zoo animals, just to name a few. One manufacturer of decals is Decoral Inc. of

Illus. 26. Here's an alternate design for interlocking puzzle pieces.

Illus. 27. This child's puzzle looks simple enough for normal play and the design was intended for just that purpose. However, with this sawn type of frame, assembling the pieces could be frustrating. Unless sawn out perfectly with all straight lines and corners consistent and the same, the puzzle pieces will have to be assembled exactly as they were originally sawn out. Compare this design to those in Illus. 28 and 29.

Illus. 28. This improved design for the same age level eliminates the surrounding frame altogether, and has two fewer pieces.

Illus. 29. This puzzle of the same general design is for a more advanced age level. Note how the background is made up of more pieces and the sawn frame is free-form unlike the frame shown in Illus. 27.

Farmingdale, New York, which distributes its products to arts and crafts shops and paint outlets across the country. Illus. 35 shows typical examples of its line, which includes many other types of decals, ranging from small flowers and butterflies to larger animals and wildlife. Many different kinds of puzzles can be developed strictly by employing decal art alone. One distinct advantage of using decals is that no hand painting of your own is required. True water-transferred decals are printed on clear Mylar. When these decals are applied, they give surfaces a hand-painted look without any visible outline. We recommend varnishing over the applied decals. It is best to test the varnish first to make sure that its solvents do not lift or dissolve the decal. Refer to pages 56–57 for more information on puzzles made with decal art.

Stickers with pressure-sensitive adhesive backing can also add some special features to a puzzle. As with decals, stick-

POINTS ARE WEAK

Illus. 30. Designed with well-rounded corners, the piece on the left is preferred for puzzles made of solid wood. The piece on the right is usable if cut from plywood, but, even then, the points will be weak.

27

Illus. 31. The stand-up puzzle on the left is 1¼" thick, whereas the one on the right is ¾" thick. Thicker materials make better-looking, more stable stand-up puzzles.

ers must be applied directly to a finished wood surface and entire puzzles can develop around stickers. See Illus. 36 and 37. One feature of most stickers that might be a disadvantage is their colored background that will show up as an outline around the design. See Illus. 37. But this can be rectified, if it's objectionable to you, simply by painting the background of the puzzle a matching color.

Now that you've got some ideas about how to modify puzzles by changing levels of difficulty and personalizing designs, consider some of our suggestions for creating totally original puzzles of your own. It's basically a two-step process and fairly easy to do if you use a little imagination.

Before you get too concerned about the prospect of creating your own puzzles, be sure that you have exhausted all the possibilities with the plans in this book. Almost all of the stand-up puzzles can be converted into inlay puzzles and vice

Illus. 32. Stencils are helpful for marking names and numbers.

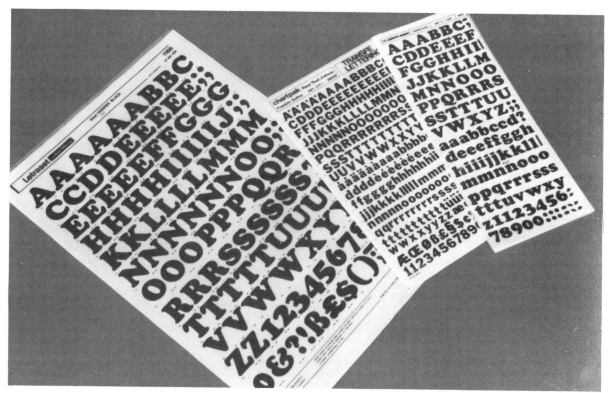

Illus. 33. Rub-on, or transfer, letters come on pressure-sensitive sheets in a wide array of different styles and sizes.

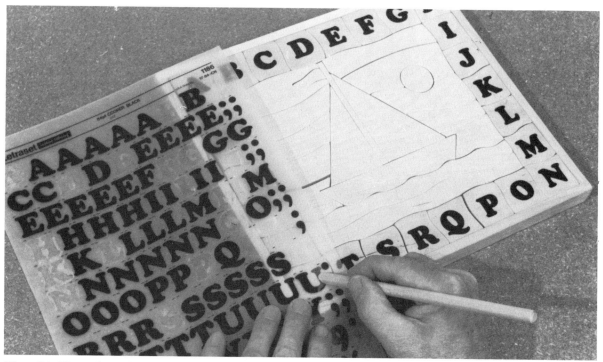

Illus. 34. The selected letter is positioned where desired and, by burnishing the carrier sheet, you transfer it to the surface of the wood.

Illus. 35. Decals come in a wide variety of sizes and designs that appeal to children. Since they have no visible outline when applied, they look as if they were actually painted directly on the wood.
(© 1986 Decorcal Inc.)

Illus. 36. Stickers with self-adhesive backing can also be useful in puzzle work. (© Dennison 1983.)

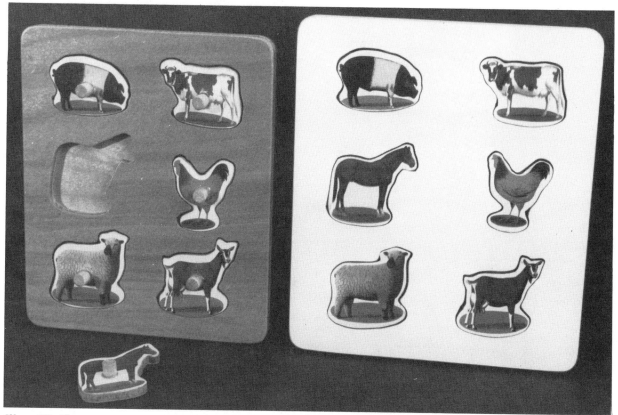

Illus. 37. Here are some puzzles made with stickers. The puzzle on the left is a knobbed version to help little hands. The puzzle on the right has a painted background that matches the background color of the sticker.

versa. Also, with a copy machine, puzzles can be enlarged or reduced to whatever size you want them.

Now, the first step in designing your own original puzzle is to determine what the subject shape is going to be. It can be a fish, a certain animal, a bird, or an airplane—whatever you want. Check various references for design ideas. Children's story books, encyclopedias, or *Scroll Saw Pattern Book* can provide many good illustrations and give you some basic profile shapes. Use an enlarging-and-reducing copy machine until you get a copy of the approximate size you want. If the design is too detailed, you will need to stylize and simplify it somewhat. A profile of a fish, for example, may have fragile or sharply pointed fins that will need to be redrawn.

Once you have the outline of the profile shape established, then simply divide it into pieces that are the size, shape, and number that correspond to the level of difficulty desired. You can make the puzzle pieces either interlocking or with irregular and straight lines.

It's best to use pieces that don't have sharply pointed areas with weak short grain because not only are they less likely to break off but they are also obviously safer for children. As a general rule, the younger the child, the more rounded all the corners should be and the easier the pieces should fit together. Using wider cutting blades will make the pieces fit together with less difficulty, but the end result will appear more sloppy. Compromise as you feel necessary.

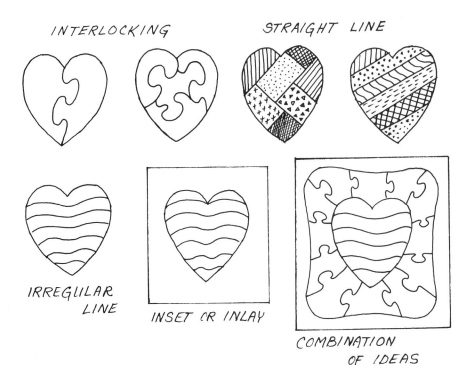

INTERLOCKING

STRAIGHT LINE

IRREGULAR LINE

INSET OR INLAY

COMBINATION OF IDEAS

Illus. 38. Some puzzle possibilities from one basic heart design.

One simple design can be worked into several different puzzle possibilities. Illus. 38 shows examples of some puzzle options that can evolve from just one simple heart-shaped design.

Illus. 39 shows some different ways of

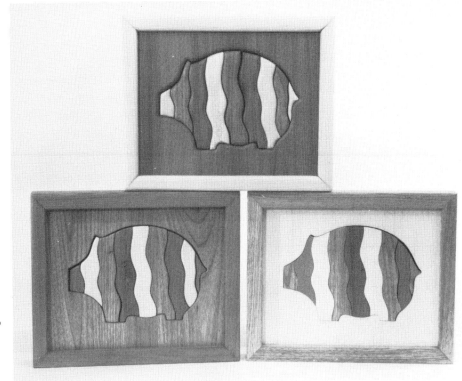

Illus. 39. The photo shows one basic idea utilizing various attractive woods. The puzzle at the top is the easiest to assemble because the pieces are rounded on the face, or up, side only. The pieces in the lower puzzles have no distinguishing fronts or backs, making them more difficult to assemble.

using various pieces of colored solid wood within the same basic design. Turn to pages 210–217 for more information concerning the steps involved in making these puzzles.

Illus. 40 shows how effective little artistic touches can be. You can imagine how much less interesting and less attractive to children these puzzles would be without the delightful eyes that give them such friendly personalities.

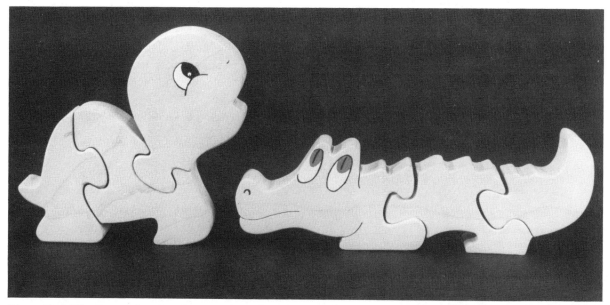

Illus. 40. Little decorative touches, such as hand-painted eyes and the use of the saw to cut and accentuate the alligator's mouth and jaw, add a lot of interest to these puzzles.

3

Basic Tools—
Techniques and Tips

This section is essentially a series of visual demonstrations, consisting of some 60 captioned illustrations, to help you make your puzzles more efficiently. A few different kinds of scroll-saw machines are highlighted here, but with no intention of

Illus. 41. This photo shows the process of transferring pattern lines to the wood with carbon paper. However, for natural finished woods, graphite paper is recommended over carbon paper because any line remaining after sawing can be easily removed. Carbon paper lines do not erase, and they will bleed through opaque top coat finishes. White graphite paper is available, and it is ideal for marking darker woods, such as walnut and cherry. You can buy graphite paper at art supply and hobby shops.

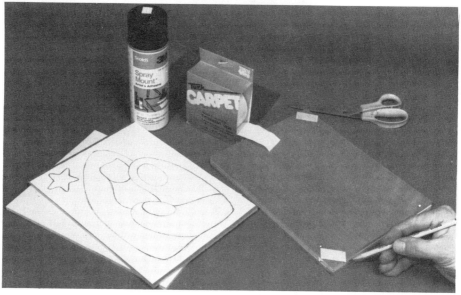

Illus. 42. When given a choice, arrange the design on the wood so that the grain runs with the longest dimension of the pieces (as on the puzzle on the left), rather than with the largest distance of the overall design (as on the puzzle on the right). The piece at the pencil point is weaker than its counterpart in the puzzle on the left.

Illus. 43. On the left, you can see a tracing or a copy machine reproduction of a pattern from this book temporarily bonded directly to the workpiece. On the right, you can see small pieces of double-faced tape applied at the corners that will hold several layers of stock together for stack-cutting identical puzzles all at one time.

recommending any specific brand, size, or style. In fact, we have tried to show how inexpensive saws of any kind can be used to make some great-looking puzzles.

When selecting a scroll saw for puzzle work, you must consider its thickness-cutting capacity and its ability to make piercing cuts inside openings. If you intend to make stand-up puzzles from thick hardwood stock, you'll need a good saw. However, inlay, or insert, puzzles are usually made from ¼"-thick plywood, which

can be cut quite easily by most scroll-saw machines, regardless of name or price. To substantiate this, you can see how the Dremel saw in Illus. 48 was used to make a small inlay puzzle from ¼" plywood.

Because the Dremel saw uses pin end blades rather than the plain end type, a much larger than normal blade-threading hole is required. However, one demonstration (Illus. 54) will show you how to make an insert puzzle without a starting at all (cutting from the outside). Illus. 66–69

Illus. 44. These are two spray adhesives useful in puzzle making. The Photo Mount, on the left, is intended for permanently mounting pictures, prints, maps, and so on, to wood, as when making jigsaw puzzles. The Spray Mount is for temporary bonding jobs, such as mounting patterns directly to the workpiece. A very light coat of the Spray Mount is all that is needed to secure a pattern directly to the wood for sawing.

Illus. 45. Removing the paper pattern from sawn pieces is easy and leaves virtually no residue on the surface. Light sanding with 150- to 220-grit sandpaper prepares the surfaces for finishing.

will show you how to grind down the ends of a typical Dremel blade to drastically reduce the size of its threading hole. Also, some other tips to make the Dremel saw function better in puzzle making with thin materials are shown in Illus. 50–55.

A new scroll saw designed especially for sawing thin materials is the Reidle scroll

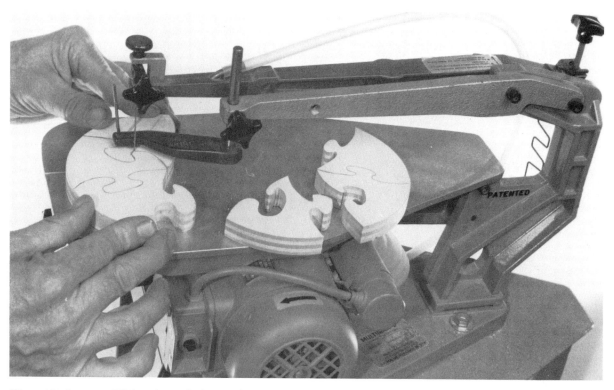

Illus. 46. Sawing ¾" hardwood plywood on Hegner's Multimax-2 saw. This is the company's middle-of-the-line machine.

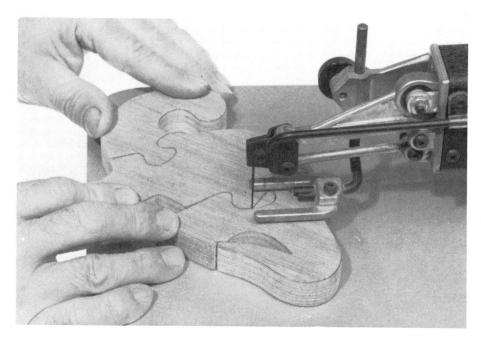

Illus. 47. Sawing ¾"-thick plywood on an Excalibur II scroll saw. With its narrow blades, this machine can effectively handle both thin and thick material.

saw, shown in Illus. 71–74. This "sit-down" model is available in kit form. The Reidle saw is intended especially for fretwork, but its greatest feature is its simple, quick blade-change mechanism. The Reidle saw is ideal for any job in thin material, including puzzles, with lots of inside openings.

The specifics pertaining to finishing and painting are covered in Chapter 8.

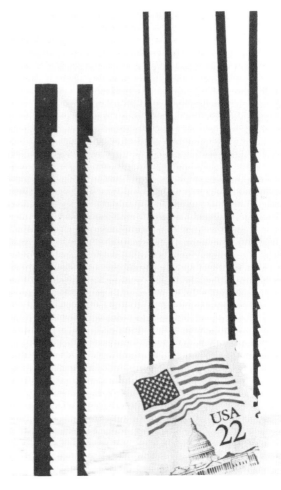

Illus. 48. These are some typical blades for puzzle work. From left to right: Dremel's coarse and fine pin end blades, and No. 5, No. 7, No. 11, and No. 11 (skip double-tooth) blades used on constant-tension scroll saws. When cutting thick material, you will need to use heavier and wider blades.

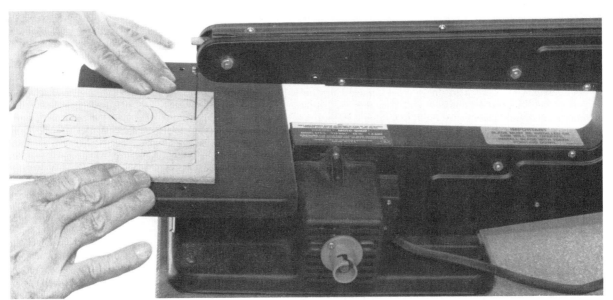

Illus. 49. The Dremel saw can cut this ¼" material very easily, so it's ideal for making insert puzzles. However, this saw has some limitations, a few of which can somewhat be reckoned with as future illustrations will show.

Illus. 50 (left). Standard blades for the Dremel saw are too wide to permit sharp, zero-radius, or on-the-spot turns, which are possible with other modern constant-tension scroll saws. The idea of rounding the sharp rear edges, borrowed from the band saw expert Mark Duginske, makes cornering easier and allows cutting tighter-than-usual turns on any saw—but particularly on the Dremel saw. Illus. 51 (right). This shows on-the-spot practice turns with the Dremel saw and ¼" plywood. Here, the turn has been completed and the blade is exiting in the inbound cut.

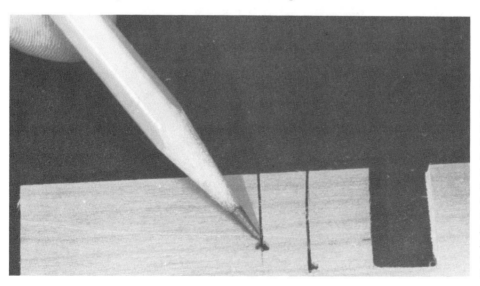

Illus. 52. This photo shows the resulting condition (which isn't terribly serious) from making 360° on-the-spot turns using a modified version of a standard fine blade on a Dremel saw cutting ¼" birch plywood. Note the reasonably sharp cornering cuts made with the same blade.

Illus. 53. Use the wider, coarse blade for cutting straight lines on the Dremel saw.

Illus. 54. Starting an insert puzzle is shown here. The cut is being made from the outside, eliminating the need to use a blade-threading hole. This technique saves some time, but usually results in a visible saw cut in the completed project. See Illus. 55.

Illus. 55. This photo shows all cutting completed. Notice where the sharp inside and outside turns have left some blade rub and burn marks.

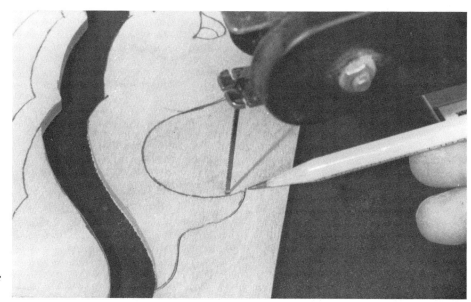

Illus. 56. When possible, round sharp corner profiles during the sawing operation.

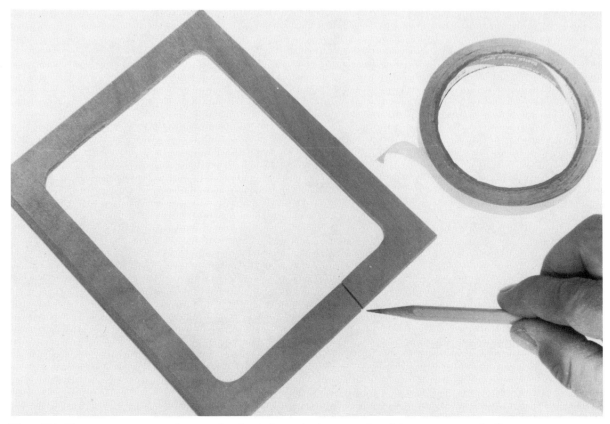

Illus. 57. Here, you can see the saw kerf cut through the outside of the sawn puzzle frame.

Illus. 58. Tape the saw kerf closed.

Illus. 59. This shows glue being applied to the back of the top layer (puzzle frame).

Illus. 60. The tape holds the top and bottom pieces so that their edges remain aligned until gluing pressure is applied.

Illus. 61. Any heavy weight—such as cement blocks, bricks, or this piece of steel—can be used to provide gluing pressure on top of this ¾″-thick plywood platen.

Illus. 62. A good glue joint should have a little bit of glue squeezed out, as shown. Spread the glue so that it is squeezed out more around the outside perimeter than along the inside.

44

Illus. 63. You should clean away the excess glue along the inside between the time the glue sets and the time the glue cures hard.

Illus. 64. Here's the completed puzzle made without a piercing hole for the inside cutouts.

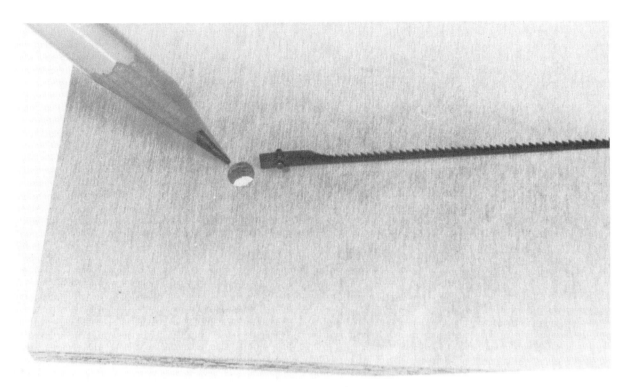

Illus. 65. When sawing inside openings or making piercing cuts, this Dremel pin type of blade normally requires a ⁵⁄₃₂″-diameter hole so that you can thread it through the workpiece.

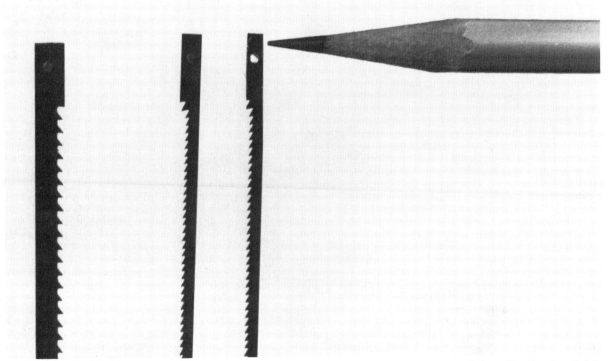

Illus. 66. Dremel pin end saw blades are available only in two sizes: coarse and fine. On the far right, you can see the end of a fine blade, ground down to permit insertion through a smaller-than-usual hole, used for making internal cuts.

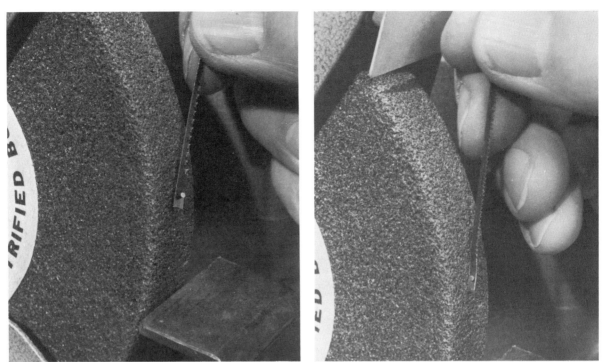

Illus. 67 (left). Grinding down the length of the pins is also necessary. Illus. 68 (right). Grinding down the blade end width of a Dremel saw blade is shown here.

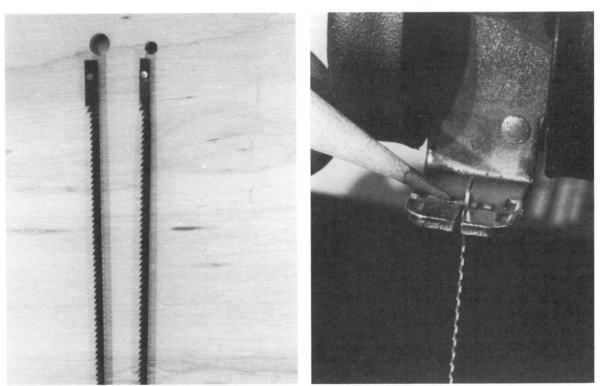

Illus. 69 (left). The ground Dremel pin blade on the right slips through a $^3/_{32}$"-diameter hole, but a $^5/_{32}$"-diameter hole is required for the same, unaltered blade on the left. Illus. 70 (right). The shortened pins still provide adequate support in the blade holder.

Illus. 71. This new kit scroll saw, developed by Jim Reidle, is designed for intricate cutting of thin stock up to ½" thick. Note the "sit-down" working height.

Illus. 72. This is a close-up of the Reidle scroll saw. Note the very fine blade.

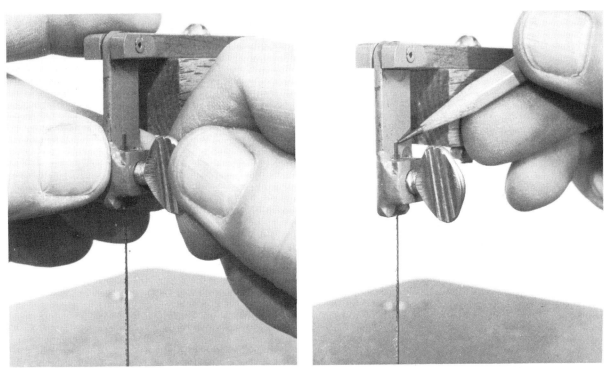

Illus. 73 (left). Here's a close-up of the simple, quick blade-change clamping feature of the Reidle saw. This is one of the easiest saws to use with plain end blades. Illus. 74 (right). The blade should be inserted to approximately the same height in the holder each time.

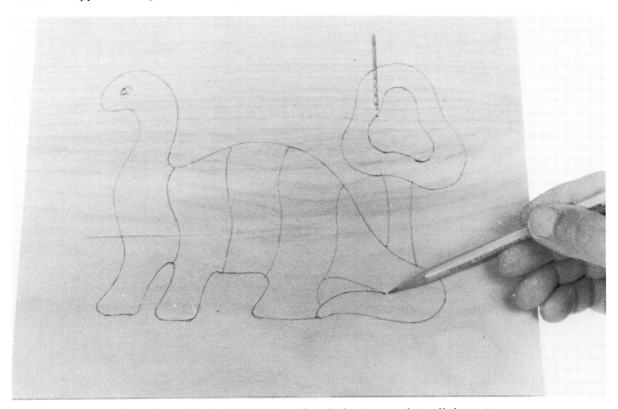

Illus. 75. This puzzle will require two blade-threading holes to complete all the cuts.

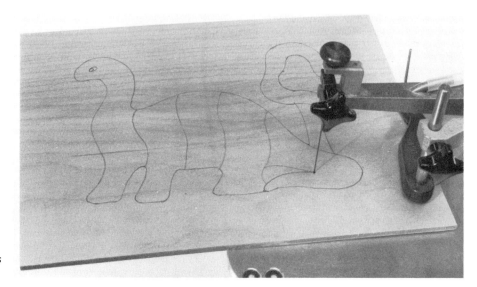

Illus. 76. When possible, locate blade-threading holes at sharp corners, such as this.

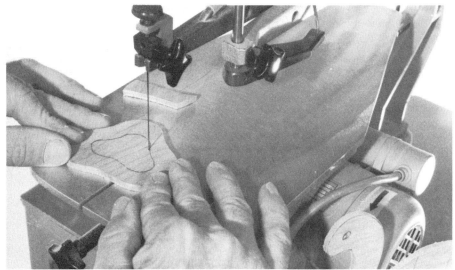

Illus. 77. Here's an example of making an inside cut. The blade is threaded through a very small hole drilled on the line. You will need to do some file work and sanding after sawing to smooth out the line near the hole area.

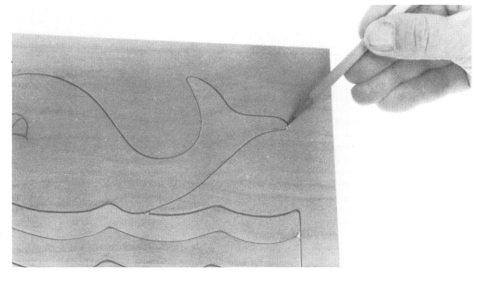

Illus. 78. The corners are rounded by sawing only.

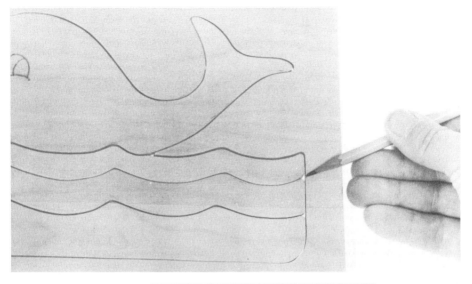

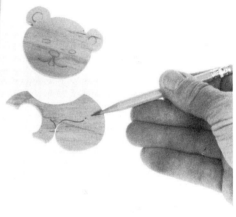

Illus. 79. Here, the sharp corners are rounded by sawing and sanding.

Illus. 80. Saw cuts often function as lines in the design of some puzzle parts. When this is the case, narrow blades and sharp-turn cutting capabilities become important advantages.

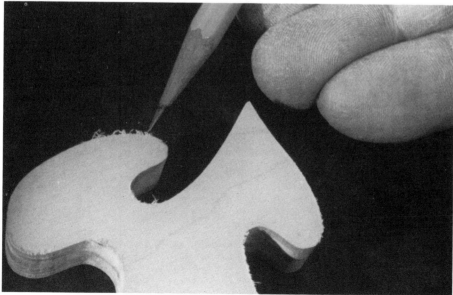

Illus. 81. Some fuzz or fibres on the blade-exit side of the work is normal, as long as no serious splintering occurs. Light sanding will remove this, but all edges should be well rounded with 80- to 100-grit sandpaper, anyway. Should splintering exist, change to a finer blade, use a better grade of material, or support the work on a back-up piece of scrap during cutting.

Illus. 82. Round the corners of the puzzle pieces with 80- to 100-grit abrasive.

Illus. 83. Sanding straight cuts on small pieces is best done this way.

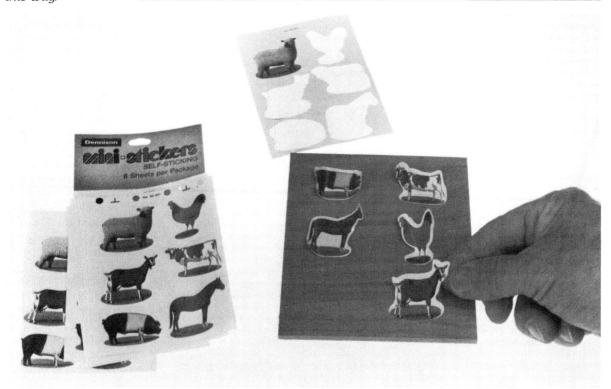

Illus. 84. You can use stickers for puzzle art. Here, stickers, with their own adhesive backing, are being applied to a previously finished plywood panel. (© Dennison 1983.)

Illus. 85. The edges of the upper form board layer of an insert puzzle are sanded on both surfaces to remove any fuzz and to round them over before the board is glued to the backing panel.

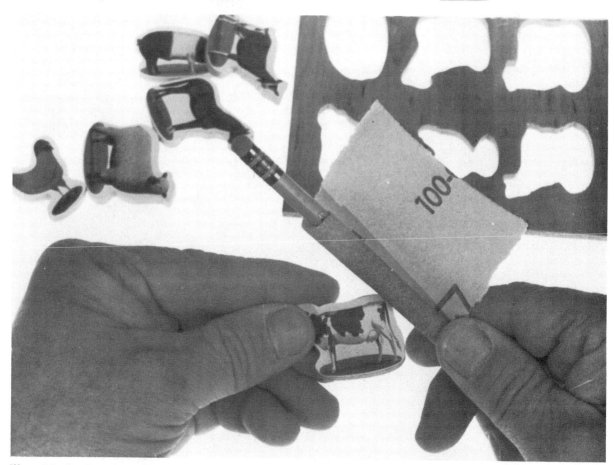

Illus. 86. So that this puzzle part made from a sticker will resist wear and fraying, soften its sharp edges with 80- to 100-grit abrasive. After sanding, spray with a coat of varnish or lacquer. Be sure to test first to be sure that the finish will not dissolve the sticker's ink or adhesive.

Illus. 87. Flap wheel sanders speed up the job of rounding sharp edges.

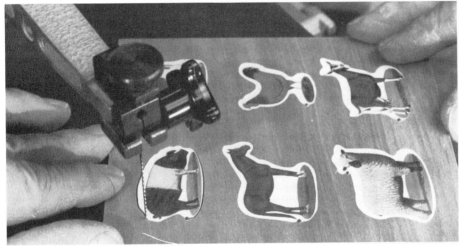

Illus. 88. Sawing around the sticker design is shown here. This piercing cut was started with a small drilled hole.

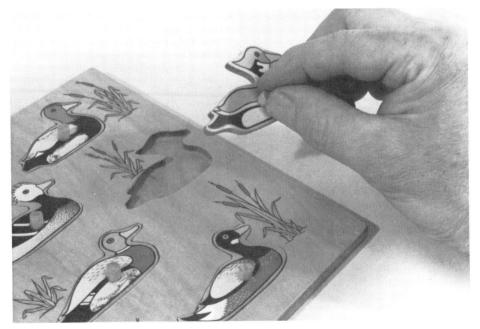

Illus. 89. For inlay puzzles, using knobbed pieces is an optional feature suitable for very young children.

54

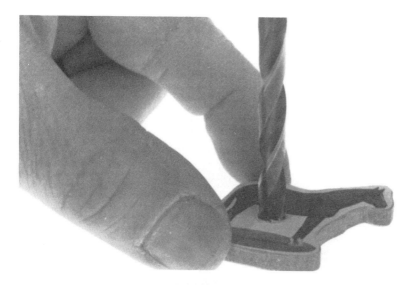

Illus. 90. Drill almost entirely through the piece. The hole should be oversize to allow room for epoxy glue.

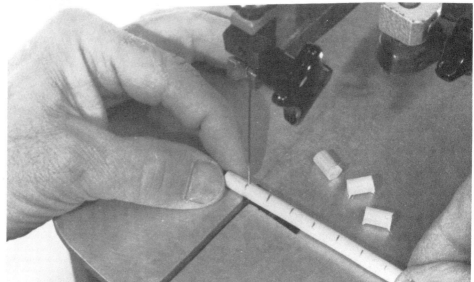

Illus. 91. This photo shows cutting ¼"-diameter dowels to ⅝" lengths for the small knobs.

Illus. 92. Using epoxy adhesive is the strongest option for gluing the short dowels into the drilled holes.

Illus. 93. The use of decals can give a puzzle a professional look. (© 1983 Decorcal Inc.)

Illus. 94. These are three puzzles made with decals. Note that the one in the middle has knobbed pieces.

Illus. 95. Wood surfaces to receive decals should be well finished, sanded smooth, and cleaned before decal application. (© 1986 Decorcal Inc.)

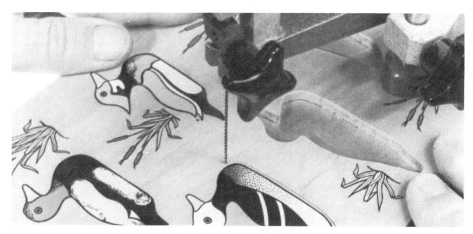

Illus. 96. Cut out each decal, sawing about 1/16" to 1/8" away from the design to allow room for sanding to ease the sharp edges.

Illus. 97. When cutting around some decal designs, it is best to simplify the cutout shape as you go.

Illus. 98. Sawing around a design is shown in this photo. Do not follow the exact profile, cutting into tight areas; instead, it's best to bypass them, as shown here, to eliminate narrowly shaped openings.

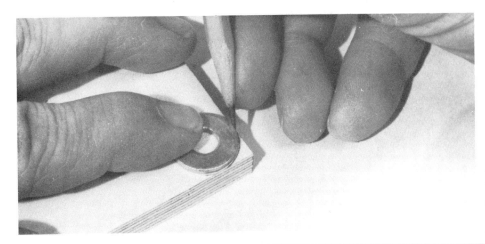

Illus. 99. A washer or coin makes a good pattern for rounding corners of inlay puzzles.

Illus. 100. This photo shows a stack-cutting job ready for production sawing. Note the pattern temporarily bonded to the surface and the pieces of double-faced tape (partly visible) at the lower-left corners. The pattern has been applied with 3 M's Spray Mount adhesive.

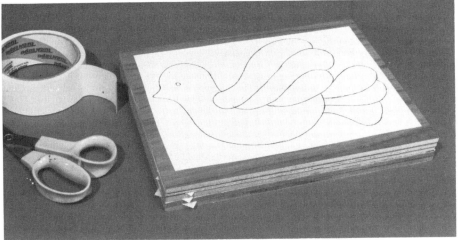

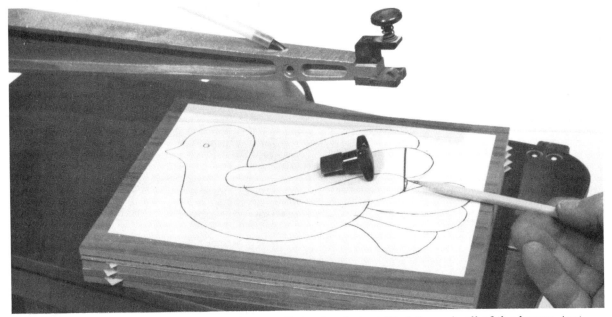

Illus. 101. The blade is threaded through a small starting hole drilled through all of the layers, just prior to sawing.

58

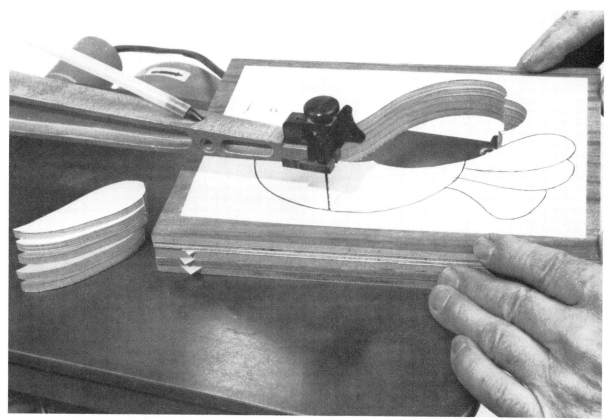

Illus. 102. The stack-cutting operation requires a good-quality saw so that all cuts will be true and each part will be identical to the other.

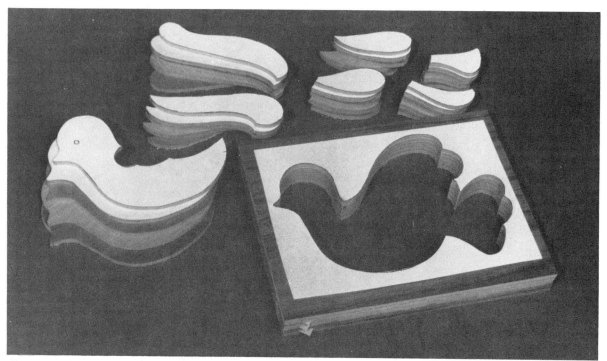

Illus. 103. Stack-cutting capabilities are essential for production puzzle making to be profitable.

Illus. 104. Removing the pattern paper is easy and leaves the wood surface clean and ready for subsequent finishing.

Illus. 105. The pieces for these five puzzles were all stack-cut at the same time. With this design, you can interchange the natural wood pieces, which were cut from different kinds of wood.

4

Making Wooden Jigsaw Puzzles

Making your own jigsaw puzzles is an easy process, which involves only three basic steps: First, you glue a suitable print or photo to a wood-sheet backing; next, you divide up the area into the spaces that are the general size and number of the desired pieces; and then you saw it into separate interlocking pieces.

Maps, postcards (Illus. 106), posters (Illus. 107), greeting cards, calendar art (Illus. 108), art prints, children's school drawings, photographs, illustrations on cereal boxes, magazine covers—and the list goes on—are all suitable material for jigsaw puzzles. Phonograph records have even been cut up and used for jigsaw puzzles; so, let your imagination flow.

Thin plywood, ⅛″ to ½″ in thickness,

Illus. 106. Postcards make good subject matter for puzzles. This one consists of six pieces.

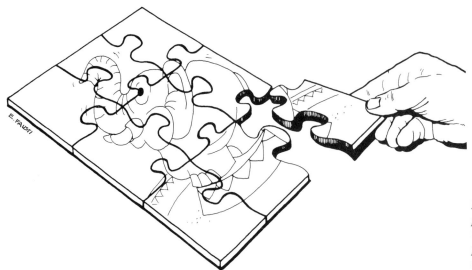

Illus. 107. A child's poster is the subject matter for this durable puzzle of ⅜″-thick Baltic birch plywood.

makes an excellent backing material. Tempered hardboard is a good substitute. Avoid using standard hardboard because it's just not tough enough. Puzzles intended for younger children, obviously, have larger pieces, and they tend to look better cut from heavier stock that is ¼″ to ½″ thick. See Illus. 107. It's good to use ⅛″ American plywood or 3-mm Baltic birch for small puzzles, such as postcards, and adult puzzles with many small pieces.

One adhesive that we strongly recommend for the bonding process is 3M's Photo Mount. This is a spray adhesive that permanently bonds paper-base sheet materials to plywood. See Illus. 109. There are other brands that also work. A double coat applied to each surface assures a perfect, durable bond. When tacky, just one or two minutes after spraying, press the "art" onto the wood-sheet material. Apply good pressure, working from the center towards

Illus. 108. Calendars are suitable art for jigsaw puzzles. This one could be used for a 150-piece puzzle.

Illus. 109. Here are some supplies for making postcard puzzles. This spray adhesive can be used to permanently bond the postcards to a plywood or hardboard backing.

the outer edges. A hard rubber roller is recommended. You can also use rubber cement or contact cement, but it's always a good idea to test them first.

With the art now mounted, you are faced with the problem of marking out the general shapes of the pieces on the surface (to be used as a cutting guide) without permanently marring the face of the puzzle. A grease pencil works well on glossy, hard surfaces, found, for example, on some photographs, calendars, slick postcards, and magazine covers. You can purchase grease pencils at art supply shops, paint outlets, and some glass shops. We use a dark one (red) for marking light-colored surfaces and a white one for marking dark-colored surfaces (Illus. 108). The latter is a Stabilo brand, which can be used for marking glass, plastic, and metal, as well as paper. You can easily remove grease-pencil marks by rubbing them lightly with a tissue.

It's best to mark surfaces that have a matt or softer type of finish with soft stick chalk or powdered chalk. A carpenter's chalk line works well, but it tends to be cumbersome when you are working on small puzzles. See Illus. 110 and 111. Of course, you can always paste a piece of paper over the surface temporarily and use an ordinary pencil to mark out the cutting-guide lines. Use a very light application of the temporary type of artist's spray adhesive. See Illus. 112 and 113.

Sawing the interlocking shaped pieces freehand will become a very easy routine once you have a little experience. Therefore, it might be a good idea to practise on some scrap until you get the feel of it. As you are cutting along, start your turn for cutting the "interlock" about one third of the way into the cut. If you visually divide up the distance, or space, between grid lines into thirds, you'll be all right. You'll instinctively make one third of it the continuing cut, make one third of the space into the interlocking segment of the piece, and then finish with another one-third continuing cut. See Illus. 114, 115, and 116.

Make all of the cuts in one direction first, either vertical (Illus. 115) or lengthwise (Illus. 116), cutting the puzzle into

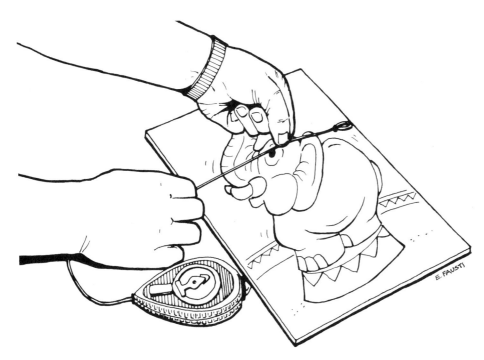

Illus. 110. A carpenter's chalk line is being used here to "snap" the lines dividing this child's poster into sections for a nine-piece puzzle.

strips of connected parts. Now, reassemble the puzzle strips and make the crosswise separating cuts. If the puzzle is difficult to handle or hold together because it's too large for the saw table, slide the assembly onto a scrap piece of corrugated cardboard. This way, you can make the crosswise separating cuts, holding both the puzzle and the cardboard together. This technique allows you to keep all of the pieces arranged in their proper order so that you won't have to reassemble the entire puzzle later. See Illus. 117 and 118.

Illus. 111. These easily removable chalk lines have divided the area so that it's now ready for cutting.

Illus. 1. Children can learn the alphabet with this challenging frame puzzle.

Illus. 2. These puzzles show the use of transparent stains and opaque color finishes.

Illus. 3. Here are some unusual but enjoyable puzzle projects for school-age children through adults.

B

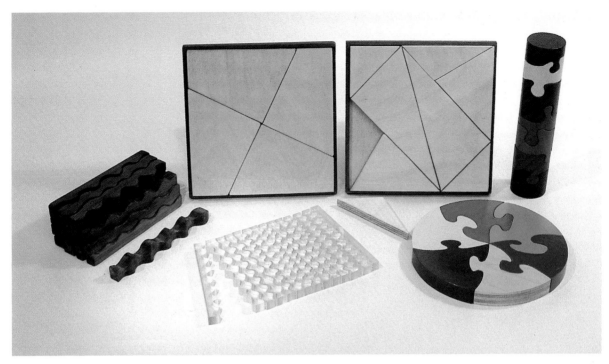

*Illus. 4. Color makes
all puzzles
more attractive.*

*Illus. 5. These inlay puzzles were developed around the use of stickers and
decals.*

Illus. 6. These basic inlay puzzles are appropriate for preschoolers.

Illus. 7. Note the soft pastel colors on the fish and the snail. The word "shapes" is all one piece, but each letter could be cut individually. The numbers on the stacking blocks have been painted on and the sharp corners have been defined with ink.

D

Illus. 8. The splashing duck puzzle has painted-on drops and ripples, Raggy Ann has painted hearts and dots, and the robot's arms are detailed with pen and ink.

Illus. 9. Here's a variety of interesting inlay puzzles.

Illus. 10. These classic designs are enriched with good choices of color.

Illus. 11. The patterns for these alphabet-letter puzzles can be used for designing personalized name puzzles in both basic styles.

F

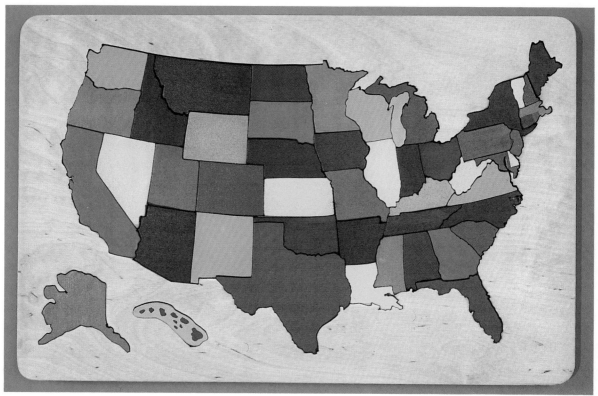

Illus. 12. Every state is detailed to provide a colorful lesson in United States geography.

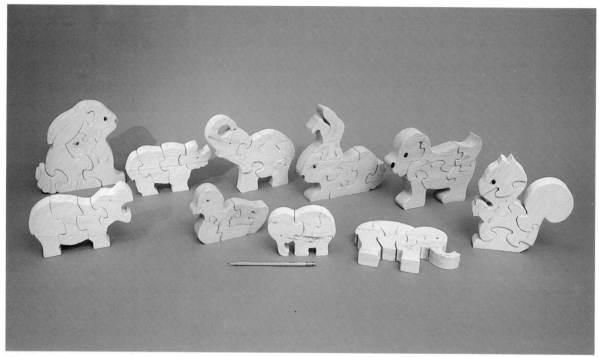

Illus. 13. Here are some typical stand-up puzzles.

Illus. 14. This double puzzle consists of one inlay over another.

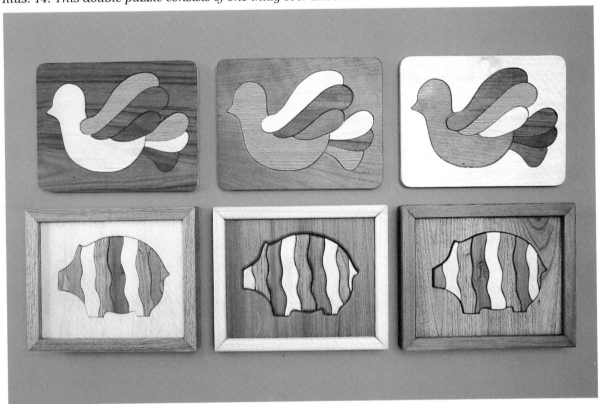

Illus. 15. These are two examples of puzzles made by stack-cutting layers of different woods and then interchanging the cut pieces.

H

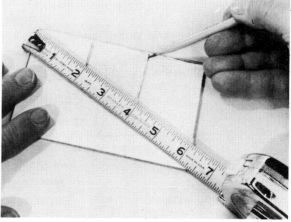

Illus. 112 (left). Applying a piece of tablet paper over the postcard using a temporary type of spray adhesive is shown here. With this method, you can pencil-mark the workpiece into a gridded guide for sawing out the individual pieces. Illus. 113 (right). Dividing a length into equal sections is shown here. Note that the tape measure is placed so that the 2" divisions are used to make uniform sections, eliminating any need for fractional calculations.

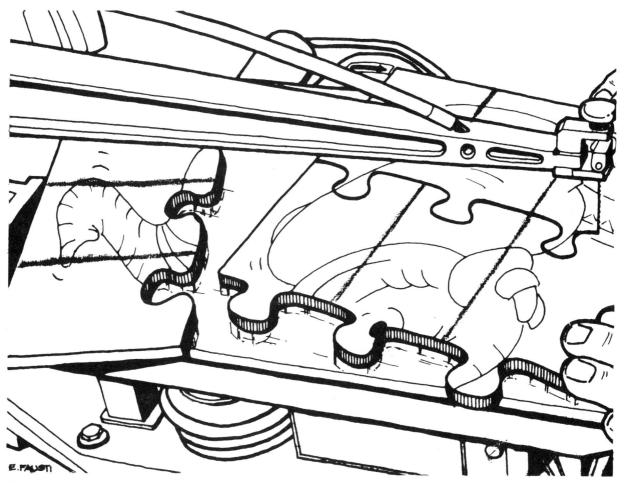

Illus. 114. Each interlocking cut is done instinctively and freehand without following a specific layout. The chalked gridded lines are only used as a guide to determine the size and number of pieces, not their shapes.

Illus. 115 (left). Sawing out the six-piece postcard puzzle is shown here. Note that the lines are only a division-of-space guide and that the actual interlocking cuts are made without layout lines to follow. Illus. 116 (right). Sawing out a 28-piece postcard puzzle on the Dremel saw using the fine blade is shown here.

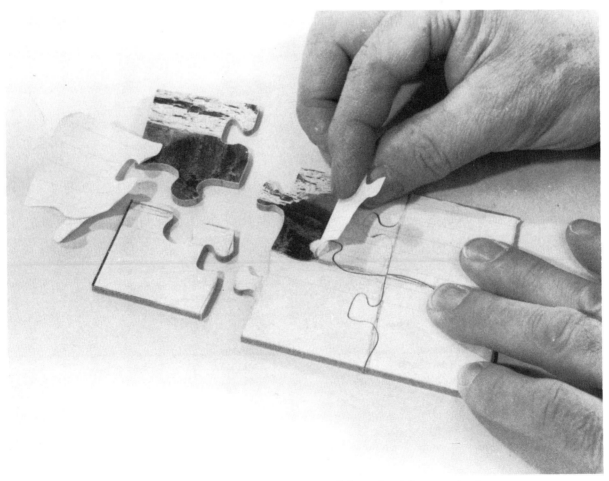

Illus. 117. After cutting is complete, remove the paper guideline sheet from each piece.

Illus. 118. Here's an assembled scroll-sawn puzzle.

5

Making Stand-Up Puzzles

Stand-up puzzles are usually cut from the thicker solid woods, but any material that can be cut within the thickness-capacity

Illus. 119. A herd of dinosaurs.

range of your scroll saw can be considered. Some of the smaller stand-up puzzles in this book were cut from only ¾″-thick American plywood (Illus. 120), and some from thicker, laminated Baltic birch plywood. For certain puzzle designs, plywood may, in fact, be a better choice than solid wood—especially for those patterns that have fragile short-grain areas, such as the giraffe on page 87.

A band saw is more likely to cut thicker materials faster and more accurately than a scroll saw. However, with a band saw, the cut surfaces will probably be much rougher.

Ultimately, what kind of material and

sawing machine you use to make stand-up puzzles depends on your own discretion. As a general rule, the thicker the material, the wider the blade's cutting path should be, but within reason. You want puzzles that fit together and come apart easily, but do not impart a look of sloppy workmanship.

This section of the book includes three stand-up puzzles that are designed so that their pieces slip over a vertical supporting dowel.

Two other types of stand-up puzzles are included in Chapter 7. One is sawn from a round wooden dowel, and the other is a circular disc sawn from plywood.

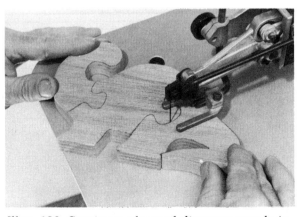

Illus. 120. Sawing a plywood dinosaur puzzle is shown here.

Illus. 121. Patterns for small dinosaurs.

Illus. 122. Patterns for small dinosaurs.

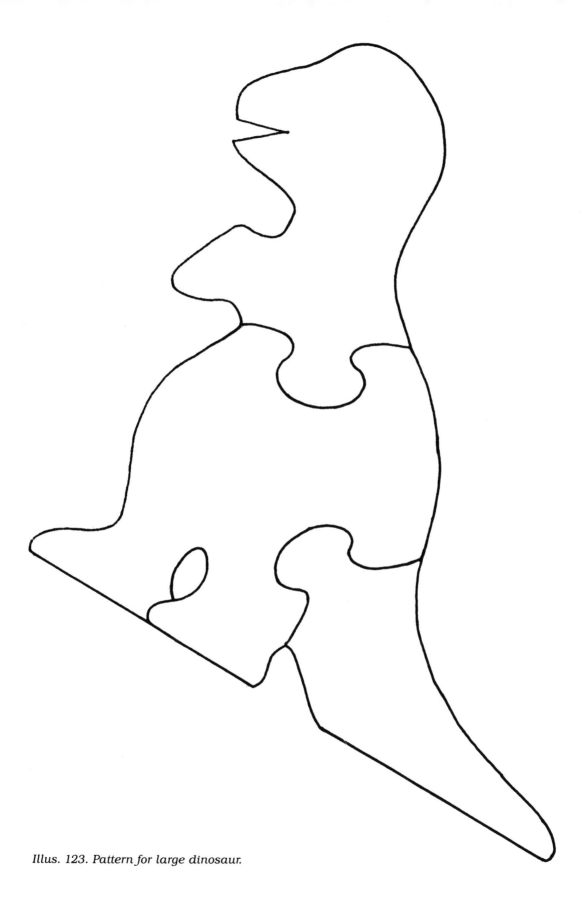

Illus. 123. Pattern for large dinosaur.

Illus. 124. Pattern for large dinosaur.

Illus. 125. Pattern for large dinosaur.

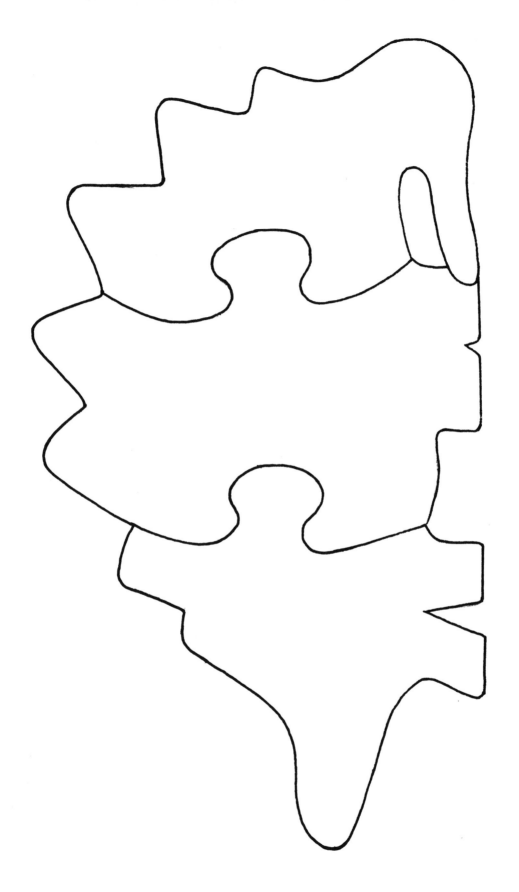

Illus. 126. Pattern for large dinosaur.

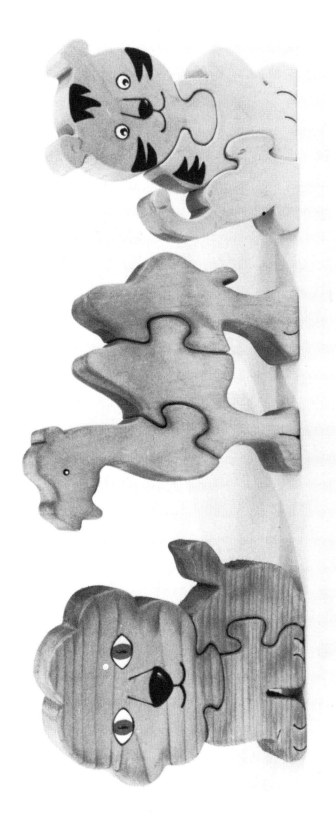

Illus. 127. A lion, camel, and tiger.

Illus. 128 (left). Tiger pattern. Illus. 129 (right). Lion pattern.

Illus. 130. Camel pattern.

Illus. 131. A happy snail and a friendly mouse.

Illus. 132. Snail pattern.

Illus. 133. Mouse pattern.

Illus. 134. A snowman and a tree.

Illus. 135. Tree pattern.

Illus. 136. Snowman pattern.

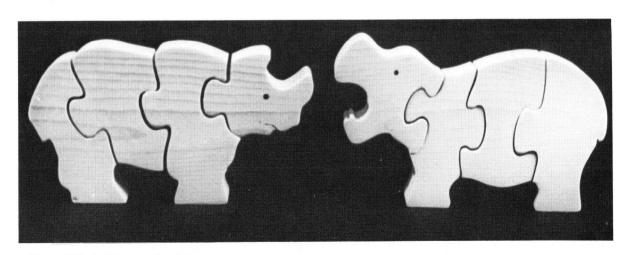

Illus. 137. A rhino and a hippo.

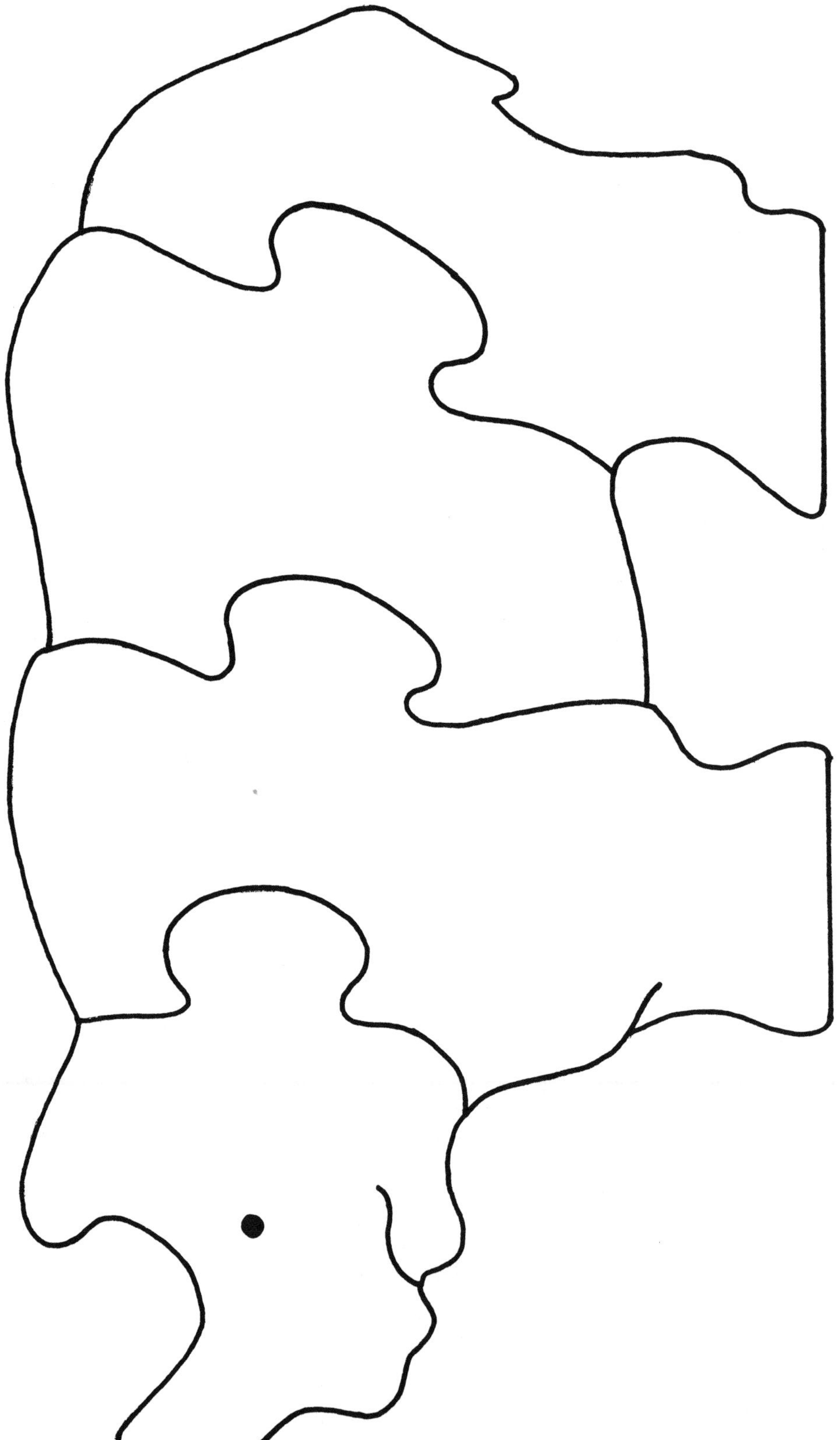

Illus. 138. Rhino pattern.

Illus. 139. Hippo pattern.

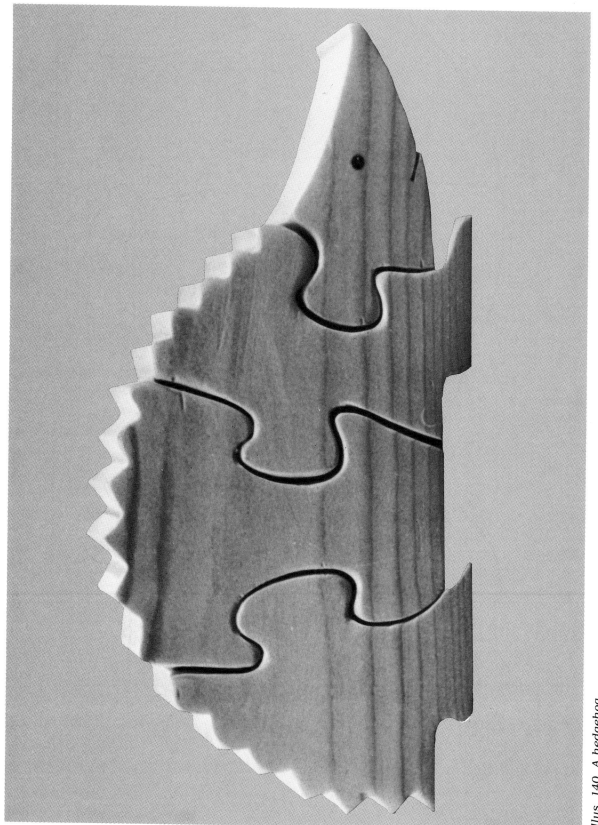

Illus. 140. A hedgehog.

Illus. 141. Hedgehog pattern.

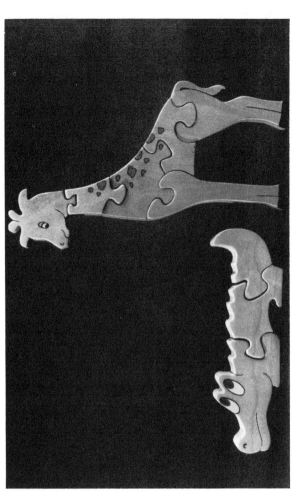

Illus. 142. A friendly alligator and a playful giraffe. Note the eye expressions.

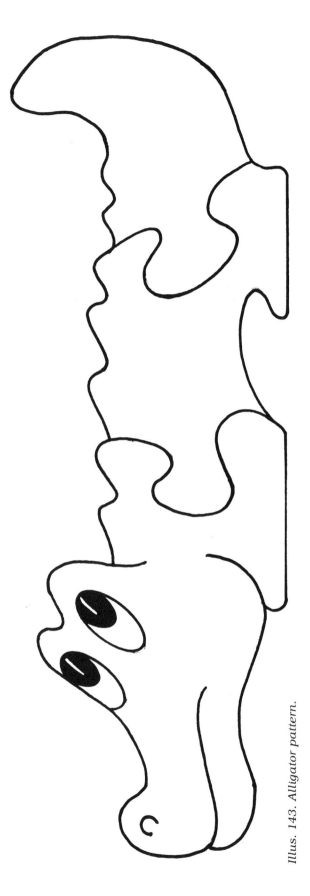

Illus. 143. Alligator pattern.

Illus. 144. Giraffe pattern.

Illus. 145. A little turtle, baby bear, and woolly sheep.

Illus. 146. Turtle pattern.

Illus. 147. Bear pattern.

Illus. 148. Lamb pattern.

Illus. 149. An elephant family.

Illus. 150. Pattern for small elephant.

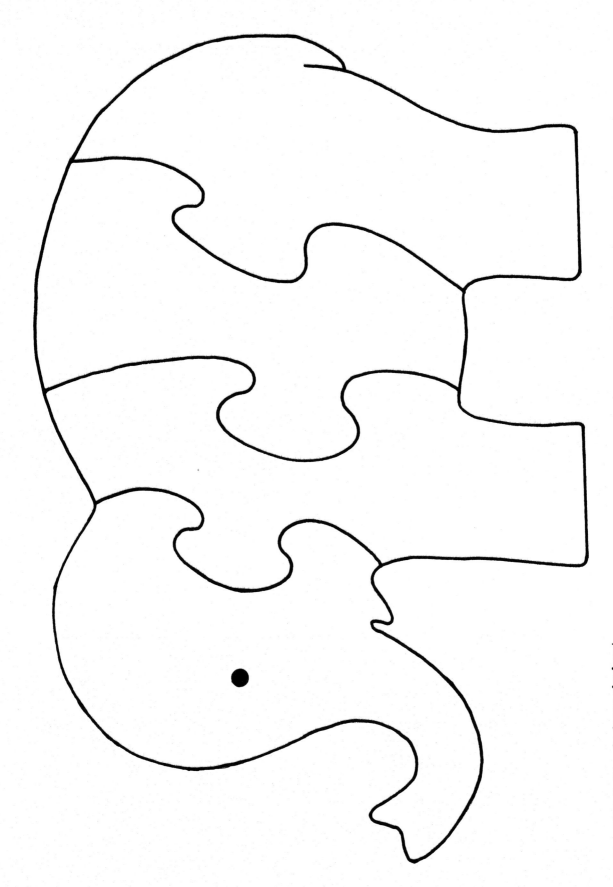

Illus. 151. Pattern for large elephant.

Illus. 152. Pattern for large elephant.

Illus. 153. A whimsical cow, a hen with a chick, and a pig.

Illus. 154. Cow pattern.

Illus. 155. Hen pattern.

Illus. 156. Pig pattern.

97

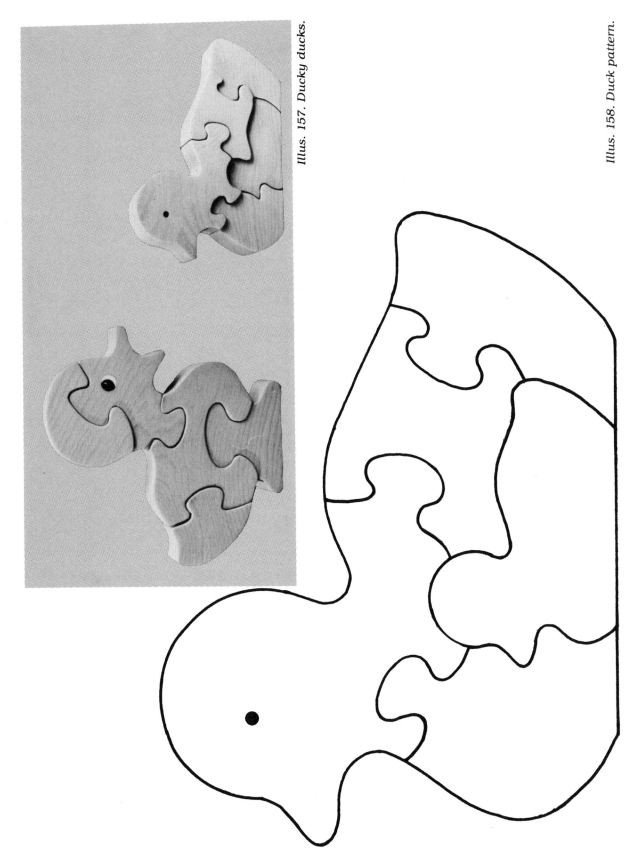

Illus. 157. Ducky ducks.

Illus. 158. Duck pattern.

Illus. 159. Duck pattern.

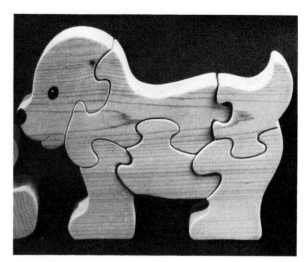

Illus. 160. A playful puppy.

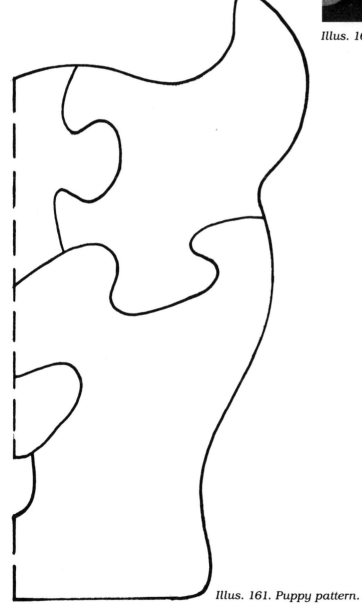

Illus. 161. Puppy pattern.

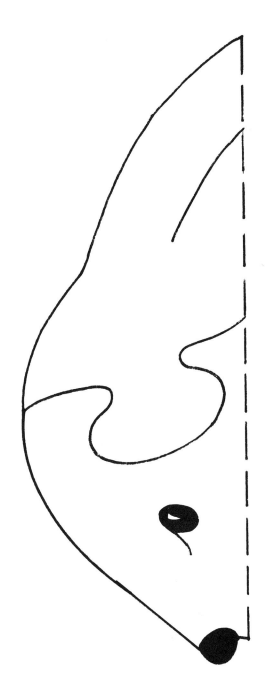

Illus. 162. A pair of rabbits. Note the grain direction on the right puzzle—the grain aligns with the ears for strength. A saw cut also defines the ears.

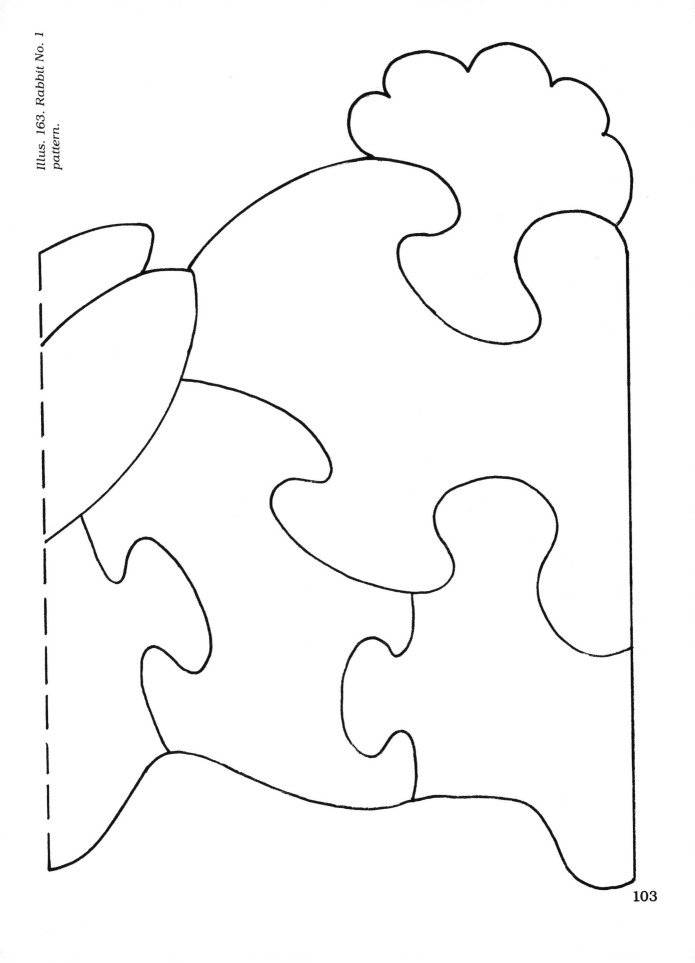

Illus. 163. Rabbit No. 1 pattern.

Illus. 164. Rabbit No. 2 pattern.

Illus. 165. A little duck, a train engine with purchased "people" parts, and a seal with a ball.

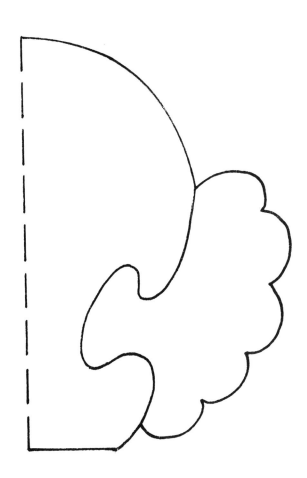

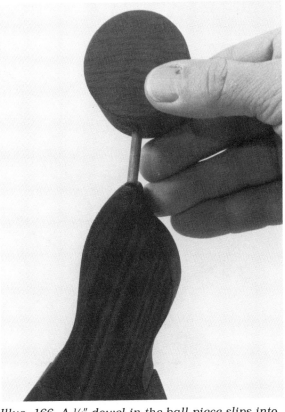

Illus. 166. A ¼" dowel in the ball piece slips into a ⁹⁄₃₂" hole drilled into the top of the puzzle.

105

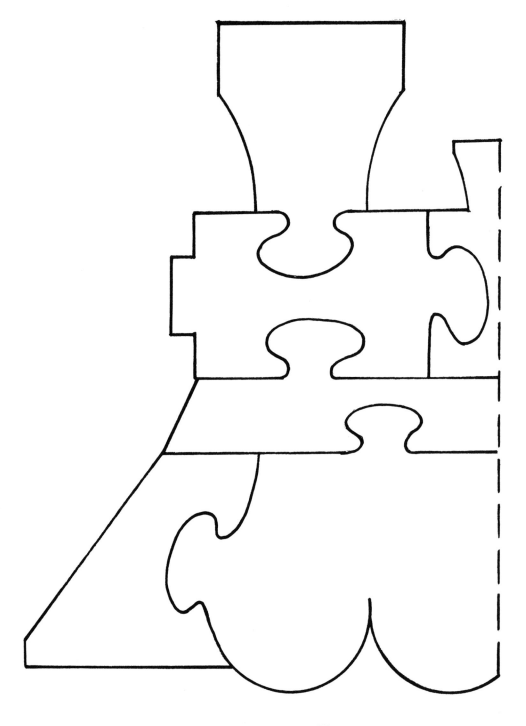

Illus. 167. Train engine pattern.

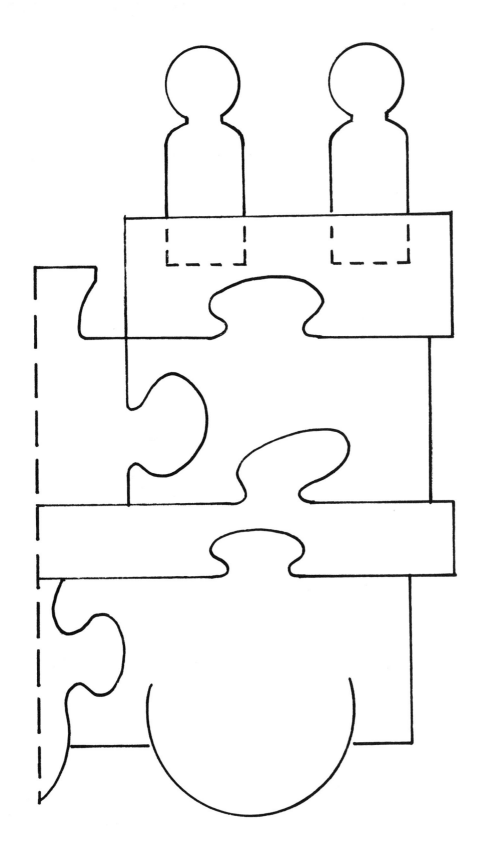

107

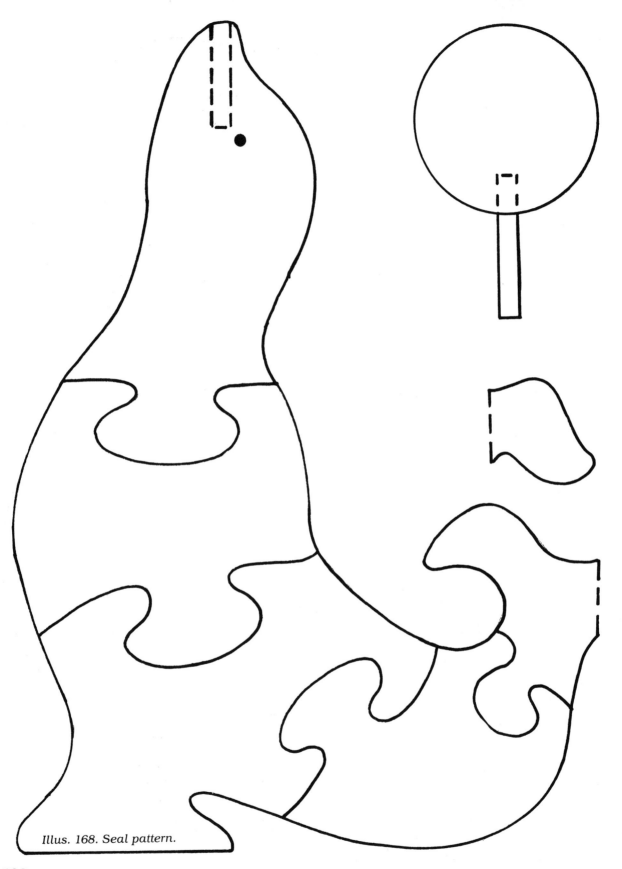

Illus. 168. Seal pattern.

Illus. 169. Squirrel pattern.

Illus. 170. Stand-up apple, pear, and Indian puzzles.

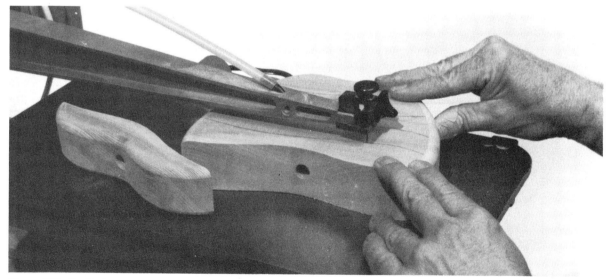

Illus. 171. Drill the vertical hole before sawing the form into pieces. This shows the apple puzzle with a ⁹⁄₁₆" hole bored before sawing. The apple and pear puzzles are made of 1¾"-thick stock and their edges are rounded with a router. Both require ½"-diameter dowels.

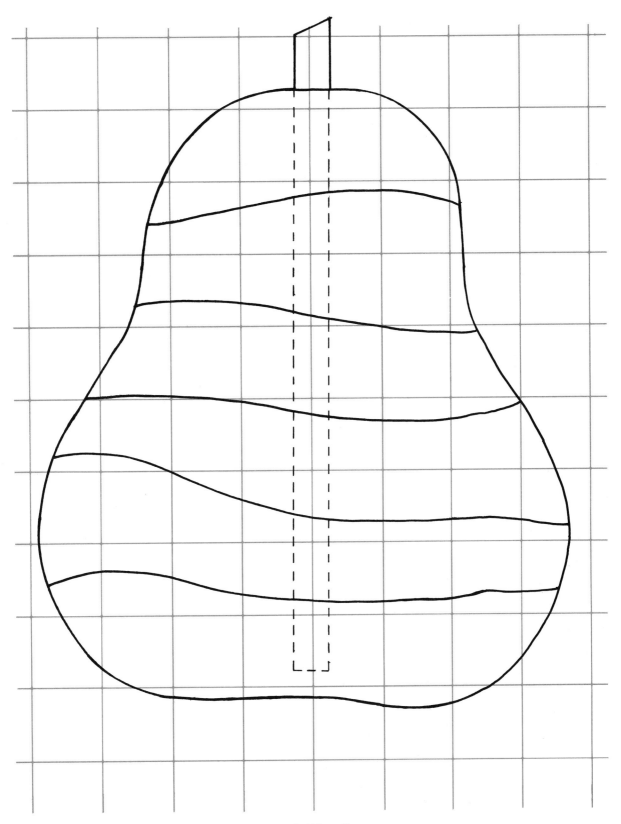

Illus. 172. Pear pattern (75% of original size, with ¾" grid).

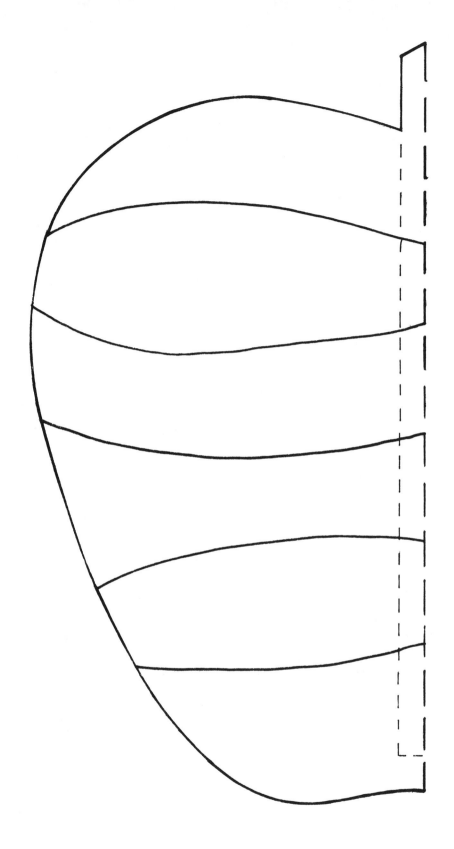

Illus. 173. Apple pattern.

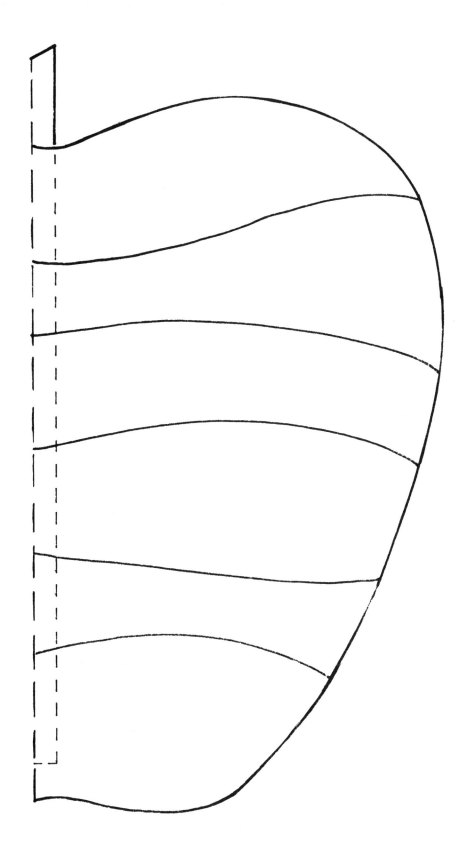

Illus. 174. This puzzle requires stock at least 1¼" thick. A vertical dowel supports and aligns the puzzle pieces. The top and bottom pieces can be drilled so that the dowel will fit snugly in Tinkertoy fashion. This Indian was made using a ⅜"-diameter dowel with saw-cut slotted ends, as shown. Drill ⅜" in the head and foot pieces and ⁷⁄₁₆" through all other pieces.

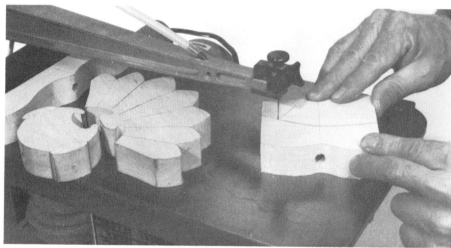

Illus. 175. Sawing out the Indian pieces is shown here. Note the previously drilled hole for the supporting dowel that runs vertically through the puzzle.

Illus. 176. The base of the Indian is sawn from three pieces of stock and then glued together, as shown. Note the slotted dowel ends and the easy slip fit that are necessary for all pieces excluding the head and base pieces that have smaller holes.

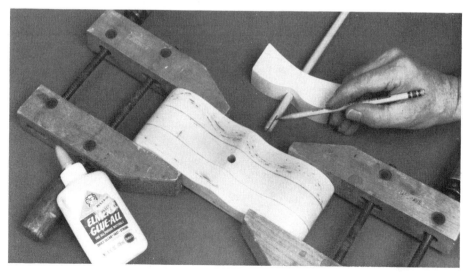

114

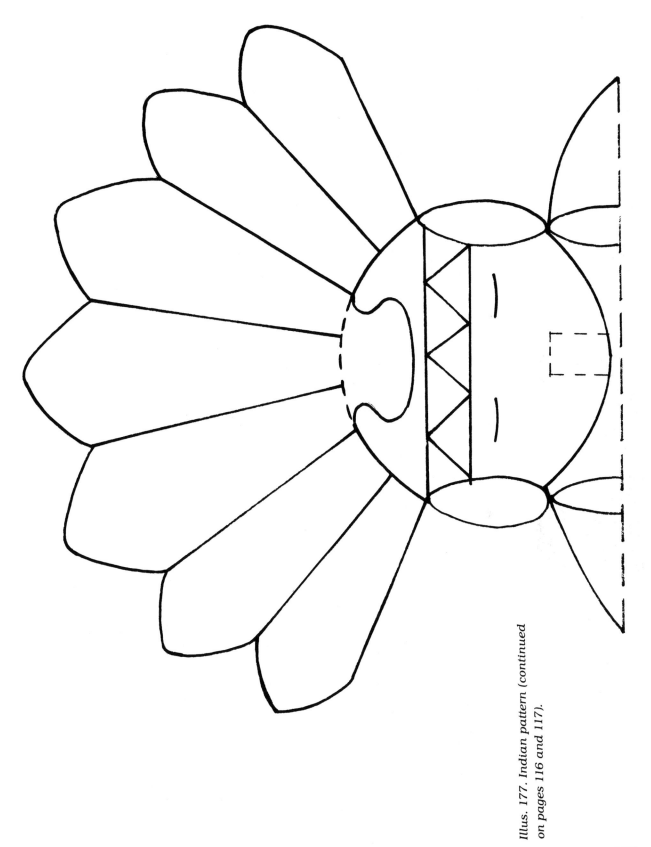

Illus. 177. Indian pattern (continued on pages 116 and 117).

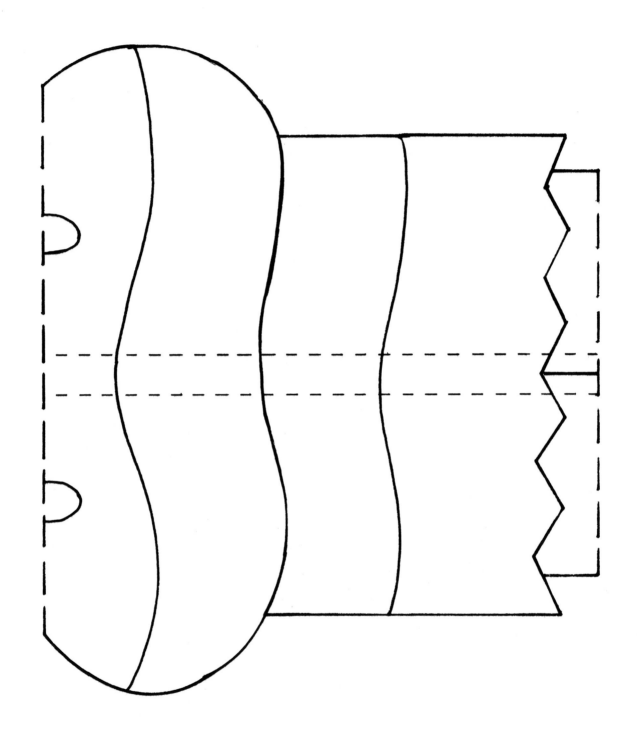

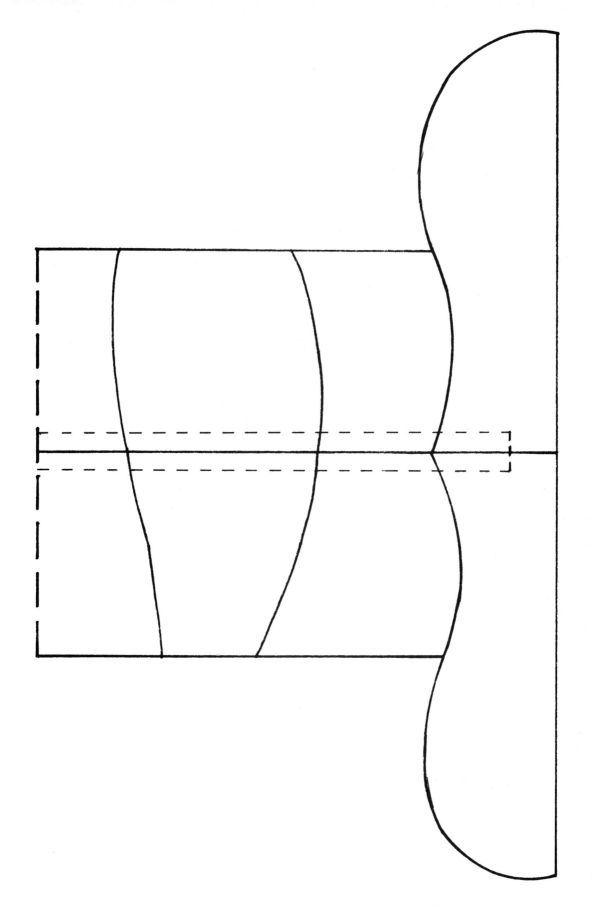

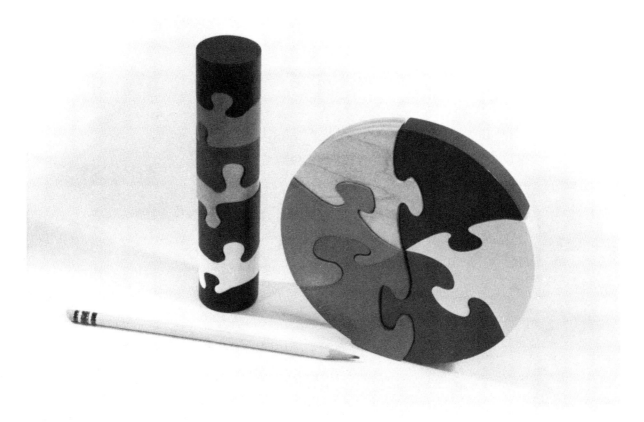

Illus. 178. These two tricky stand-up puzzles are discussed in Chapter 7.

6

Making Inlay Puzzles

Inlay puzzles—also called insert, tray, or frame, as mentioned earlier—are made from two layers of thin sheet material. The puzzle pieces are cut out of the top layer, and the remaining stock is glued permanently on top of the backing layer.

Better-quality hardwood plywood, such as ¼"-thick domestic or Baltic birch, is often used for the top layer. Inexpensive material—such as lauan, fir, or hardboard—can be used for the backing layer if it's necessary to reduce costs. Cheaper inlay puzzles are made using lower grade and thinner sheet materials. Higher quality puzzles are made of good material throughout, and they are expertly crafted and finished. All sharp edges and corners are sanded well and rounded for safety and durability. Sharp corners do not hold finishes nor do they wear well, and they may also splinter with aggressive use.

It's fairly easy to mass-produce inlay puzzles employing stack-cutting techniques. You need a scroll saw with good cutting characteristics and a thickness-cutting capacity of 1½" to 2". However, you can use almost any kind of scroll saw if you are making only one or two inlay puzzles at a time because the materials used are normally very easy to cut.

Many of the designs and patterns for the inlay puzzles that appear on the following pages can be made easier or more difficult for children to assemble. This is done by combining individual pieces so that the puzzle has larger and fewer pieces, or conversely, by dividing pieces so that it has smaller but more pieces. By studying the accompanying photographs, you will be able to see where we made our piecing cuts.

If you have access to a copy machine, it is easiest to temporarily bond a full-size copy of the pattern directly to the workpiece. Otherwise, you'll need to make a tracing of the pattern and then either secure it to the workpiece or transfer the pattern lines to the wood with carbon or graphite paper.

Refer to Chapter 8 for techniques and tips pertaining to finishing and painting puzzles.

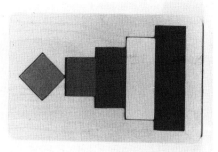

Illus. 179. This stacking-blocks inlay puzzle measures 6¾" wide by 10½" high.

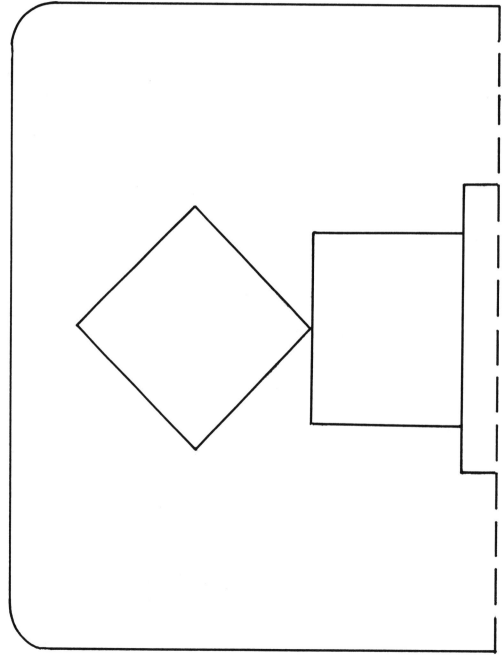

Illus. 181. The tulips puzzle is 8½" wide by 11" high. The stems are painted parts, as opposed to being cut out, making five puzzle pieces altogether.

122

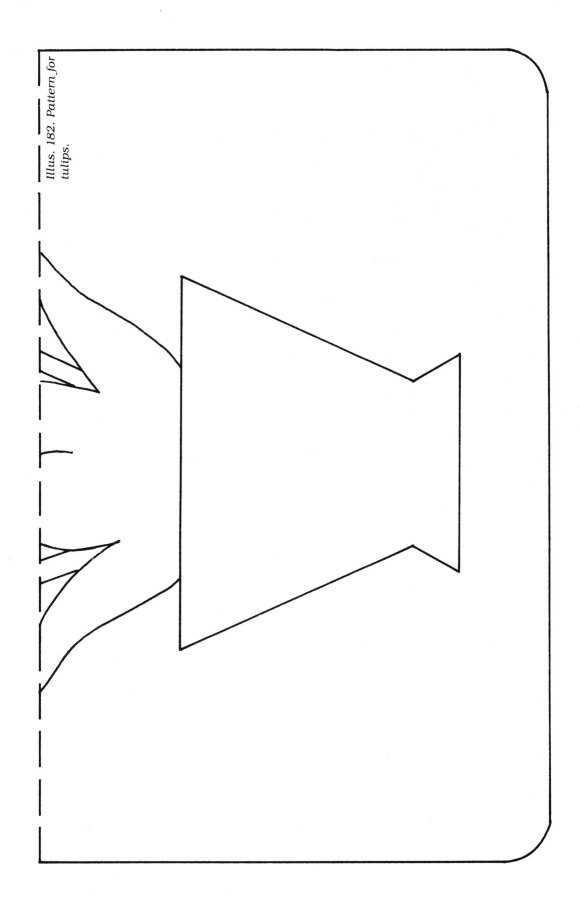

Illus. 182. Pattern for tulips.

Illus. 183. The small whale puzzle has six pieces and measures 5⅞″ × 7¼″. The larger one has only four pieces and measures 8″ wide × 10½″ long.

Illus. 184. Pattern for small whale.

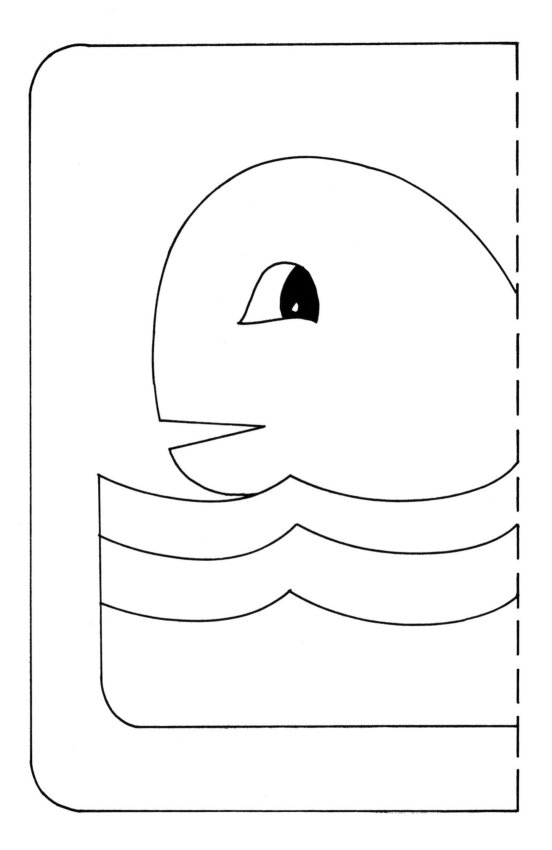

Illus. 185. Pattern for larger whale.

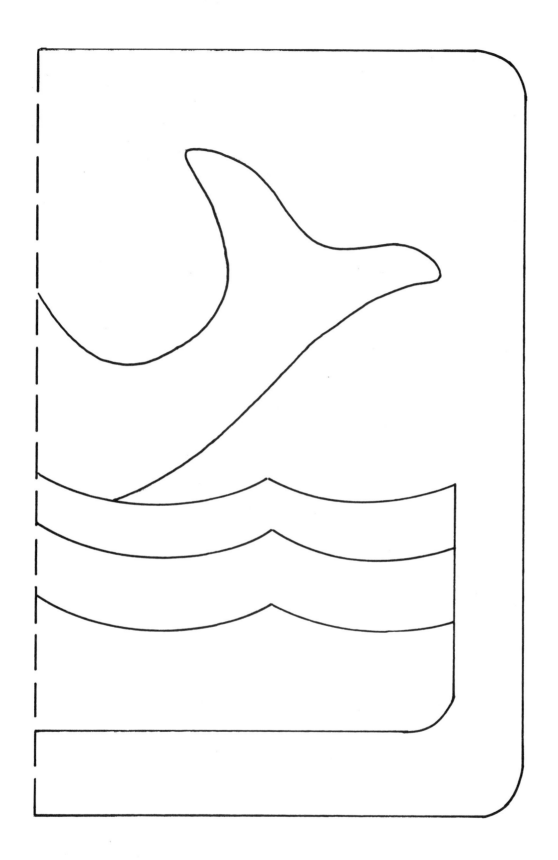

127

Illus. 186. This rainbow heart consists of six pieces in a 7¾″ × 7¾″ panel.

128

Illus. 187. Heart pattern.

Illus. 188. The eight-piece rainbow apple puzzle is 8″ wide by 8¾″ high. Note the well-rounded corners.

Illus. 189. Apple pattern.

Illus. 190. This colorful eight-piece dinosaur puzzle is 8¾" × 11½" overall.

Illus. 191. Dinosaur pattern.

132

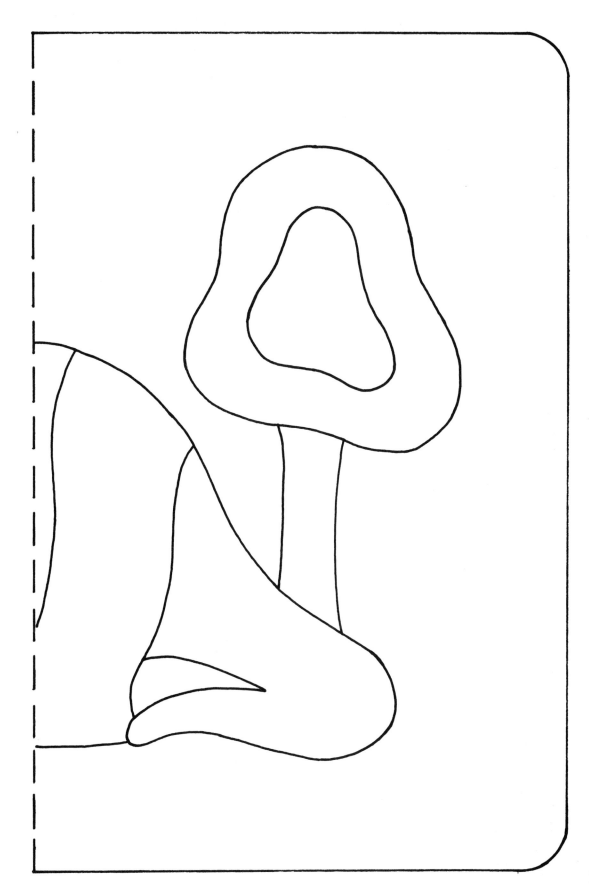

133

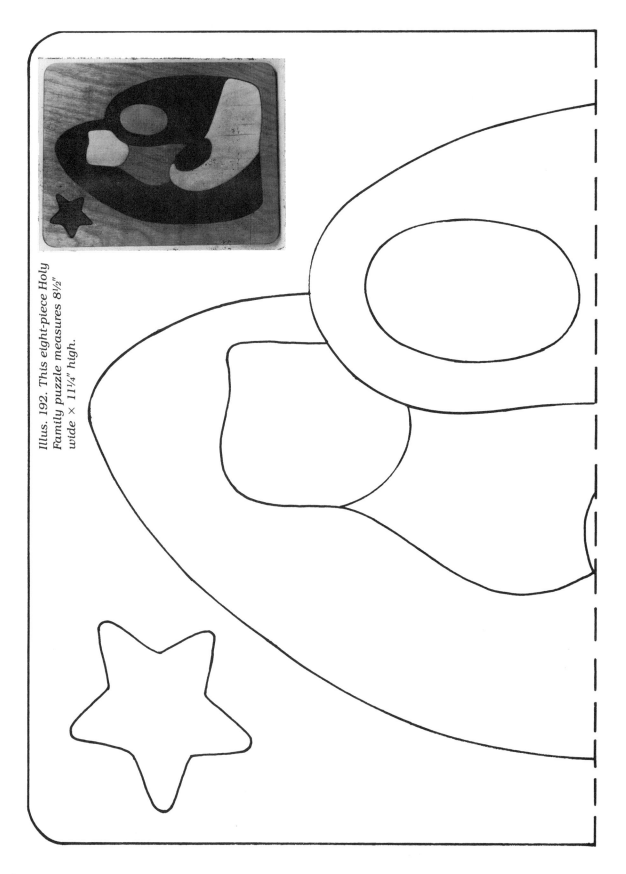

Illus. 192. This eight-piece Holy Family puzzle measures 8½″ wide × 11¼″ high.

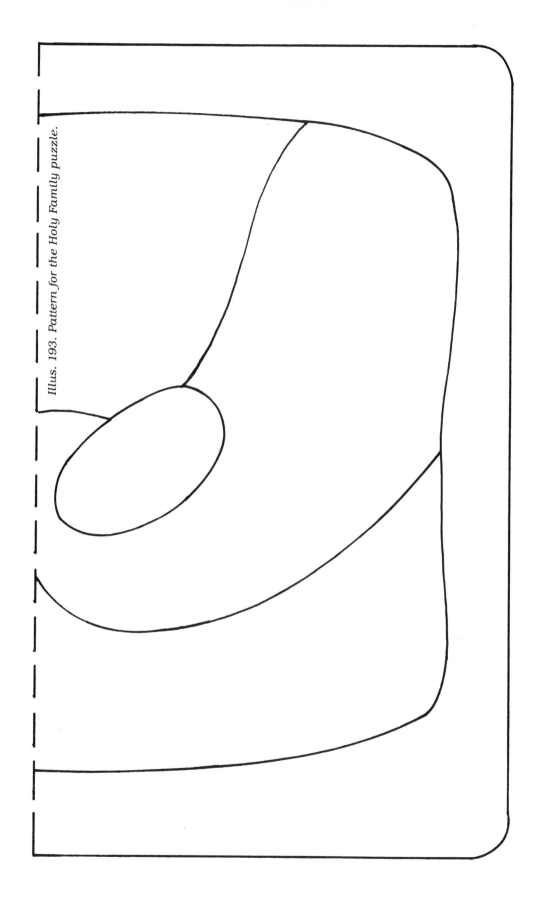

Illus. 193. Pattern for the Holy Family puzzle.

135

Illus. 194. This bear puzzle measures 8½" wide × 11" high and has only seven pieces.

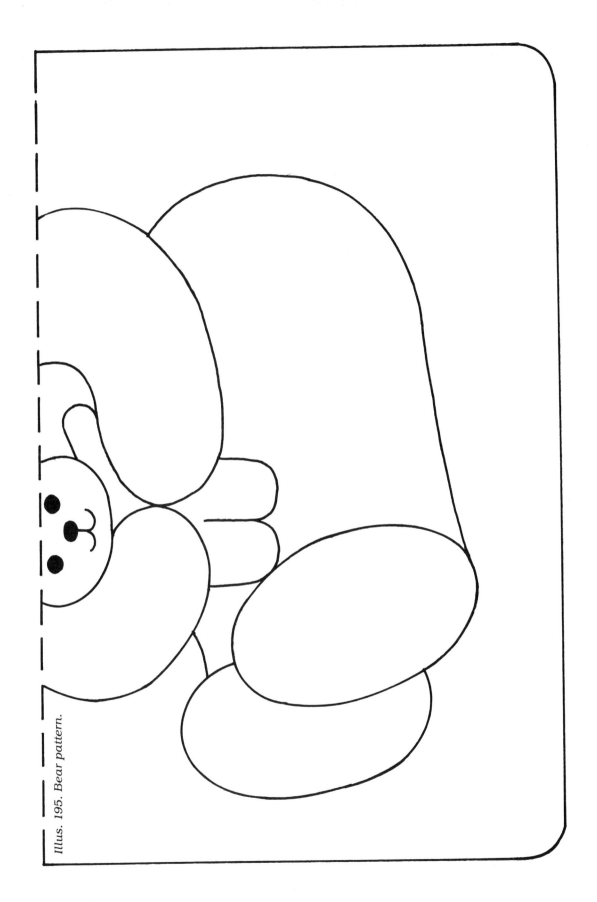

Illus. 195. Bear pattern.

Illus. 196. Raggy Ann consists of five pieces and is 8½" × 11" in size.

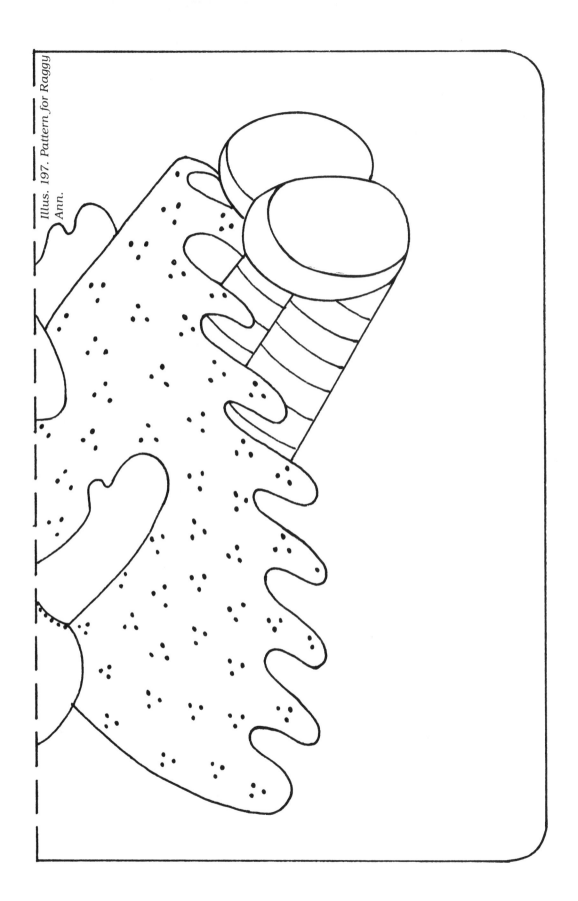

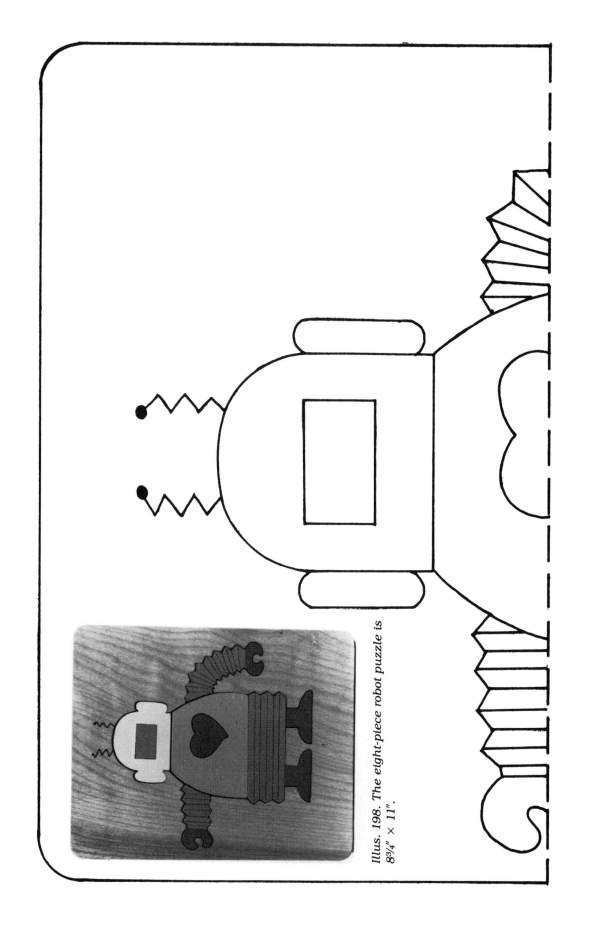

Illus. 198. The eight-piece robot puzzle is 8¾" × 11".

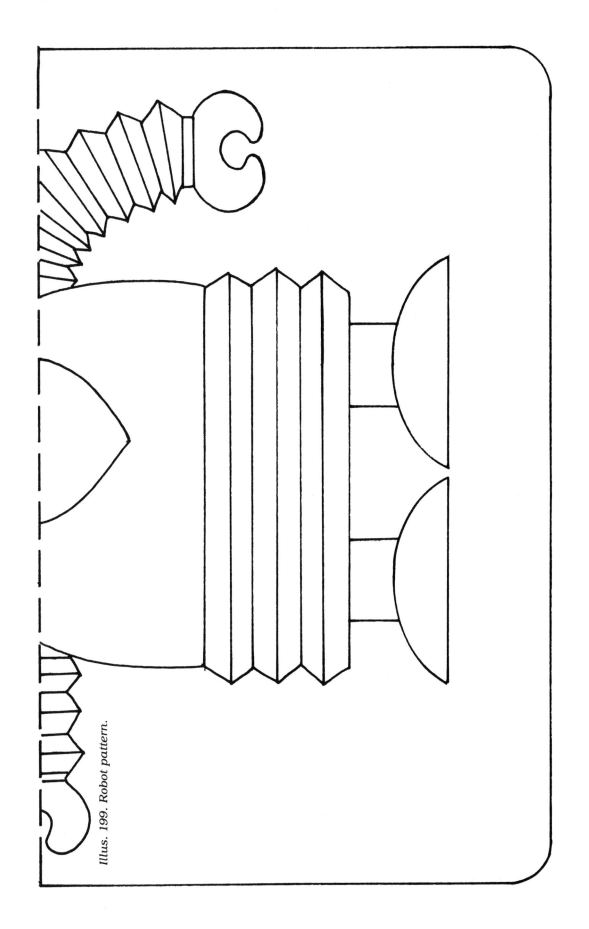

Illus. 199. Robot pattern.

Illus. 200. This 8½″ × 11½″ shapes puzzle was cut into 10 pieces with the letters remaining connected. (Turn to pages 144 and 145 for the pattern.)

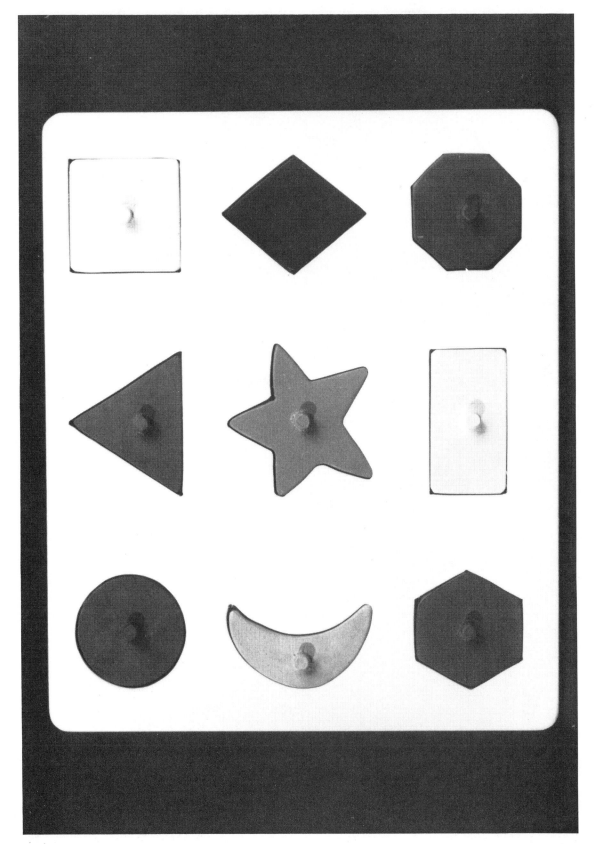

Illus. 201. This nine-piece shapes puzzle is knobbed with ¼" dowels, which are epoxy-glued into holes drilled into each piece. The overall size is 8¼" × 9¾". (Turn to pages 146 and 147 for the pattern.)

Illus. 202. Shapes pattern.

145

Illus. 203. Shapes (No. 2) pattern.

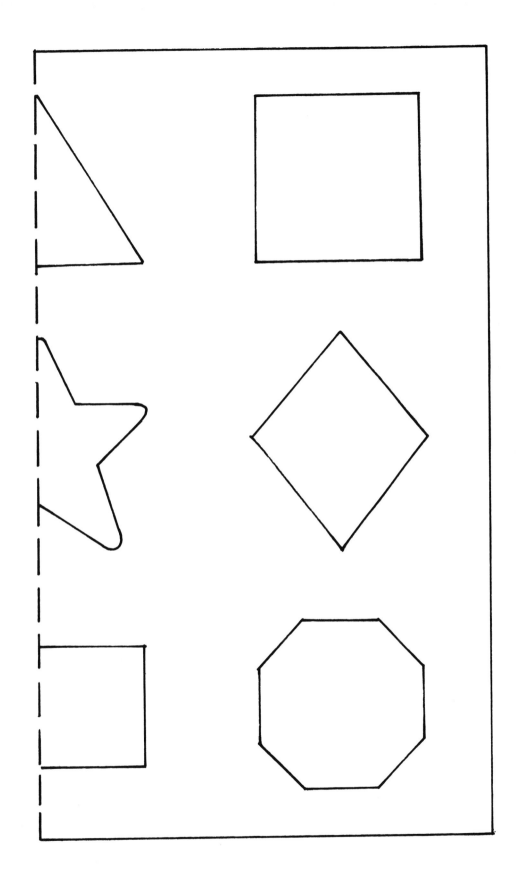

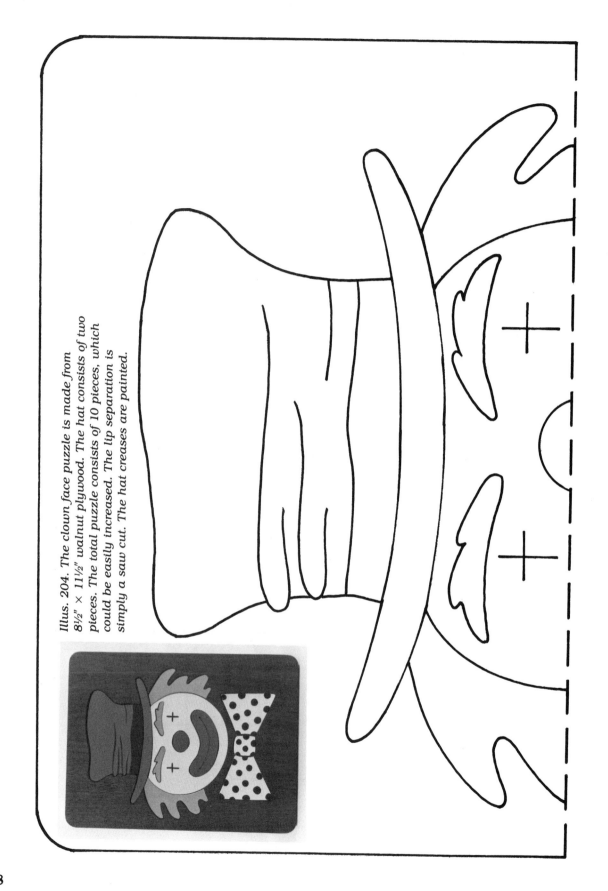

Illus. 204. The clown face puzzle is made from 8½" × 11½" walnut plywood. The hat consists of two pieces. The total puzzle consists of 10 pieces, which could be easily increased. The lip separation is simply a saw cut. The hat creases are painted.

Illus. 205. Clown face pattern.

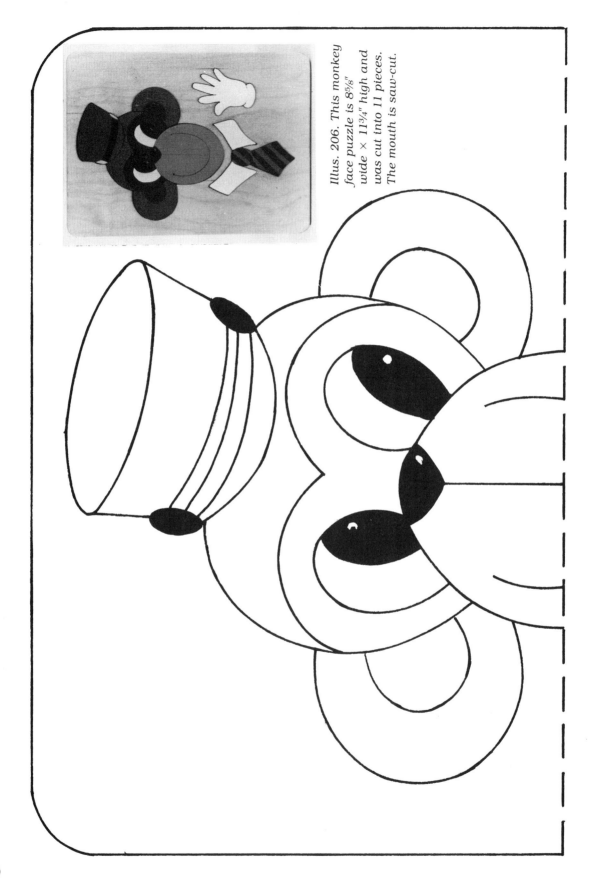

Illus. 206. This monkey face puzzle is 8⅝″ wide × 11¾″ high and was cut into 11 pieces. The mouth is saw-cut.

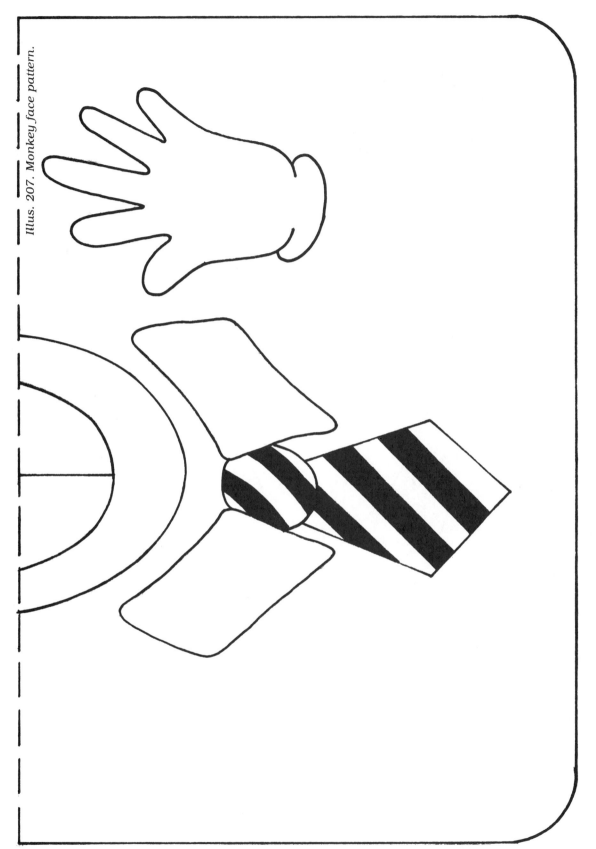

151

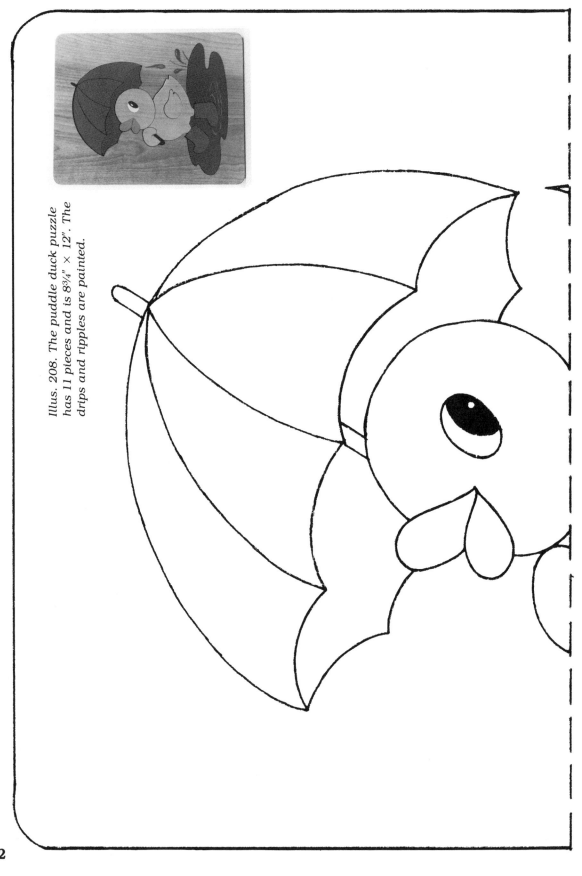

Illus. 208. The puddle duck puzzle has 11 pieces and is 8¾" × 12". The drips and ripples are painted.

152

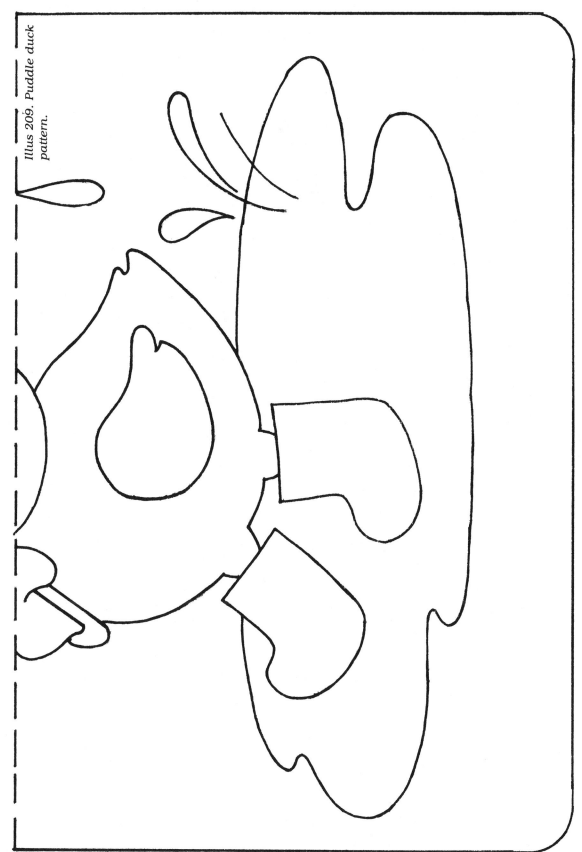

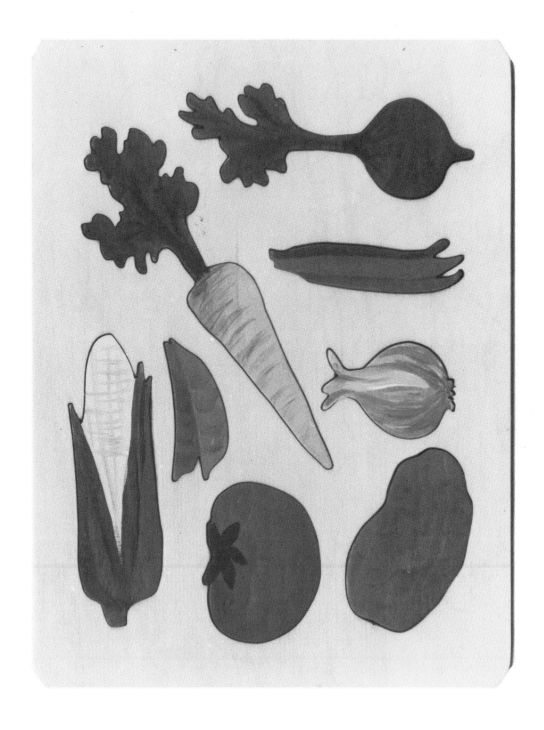

Illus. 210. This eight-piece vegetables puzzle measures 7¾" × 10½". (Turn to pages 156 and 157 for the pattern.)

Illus. 211. This seven-piece fruit puzzle is 8½″ × 11½″. (Turn to pages 158 and 159 for the pattern.)

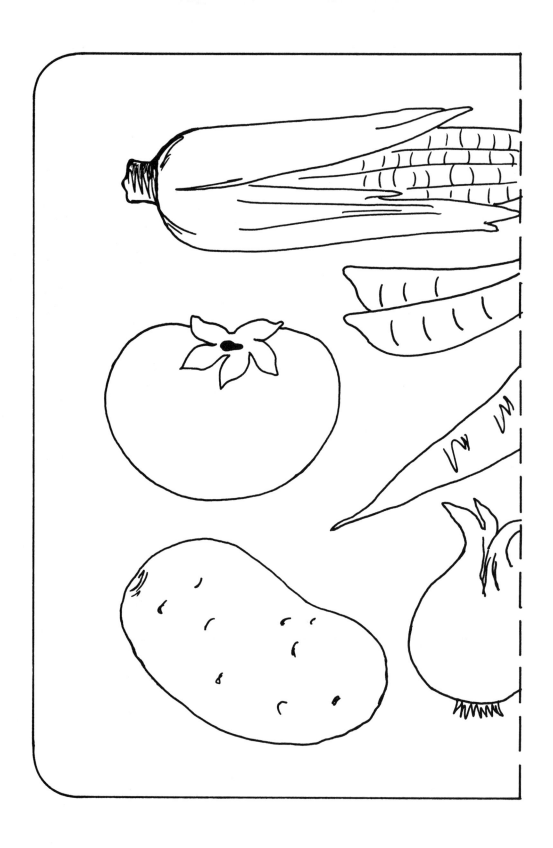

Illus. 212. Pattern for vegetables puzzle.

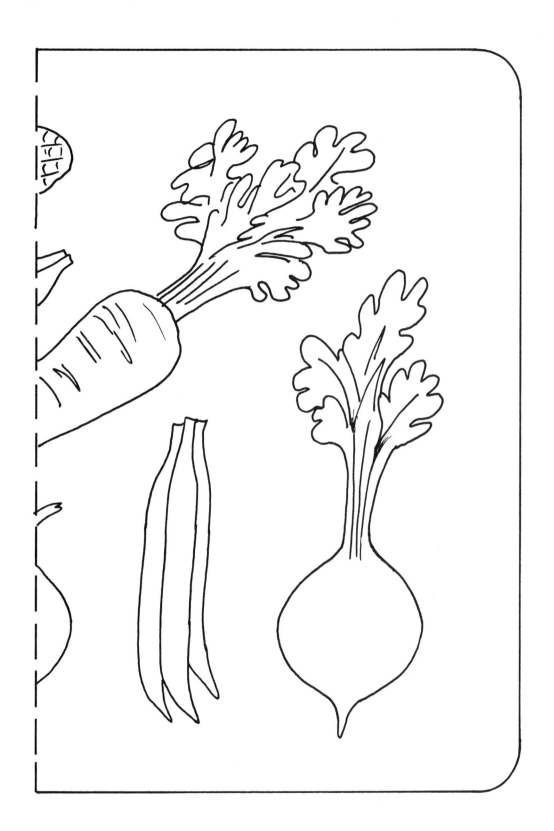

Illus. 213. Fruit puzzle pattern.

158

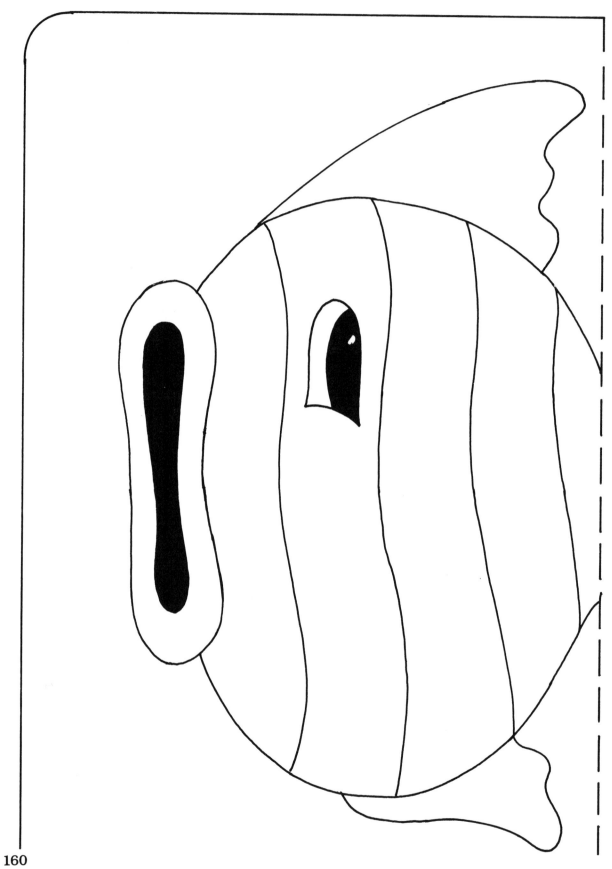

160

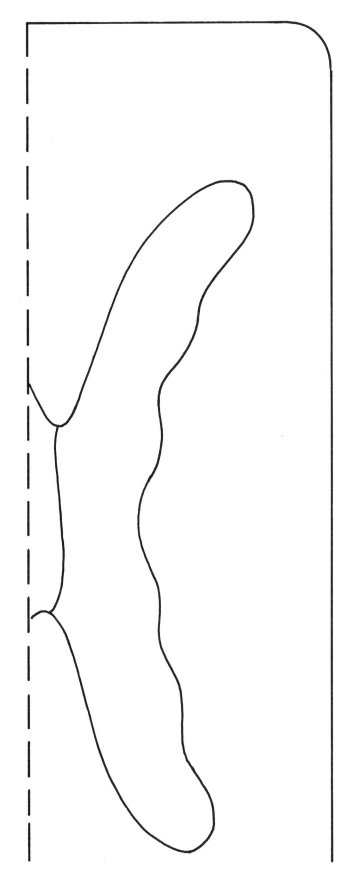

Illus. 214. This popular fish puzzle measures 9½″ × 9½″ and has 10 pieces.

Illus. 215. Fish pattern.

Illus. 216. This trio-of-seals puzzle is 8¾″ × 11½″ and has 13 pieces.

Illus. 217. Pattern for trio-of-seals puzzle.

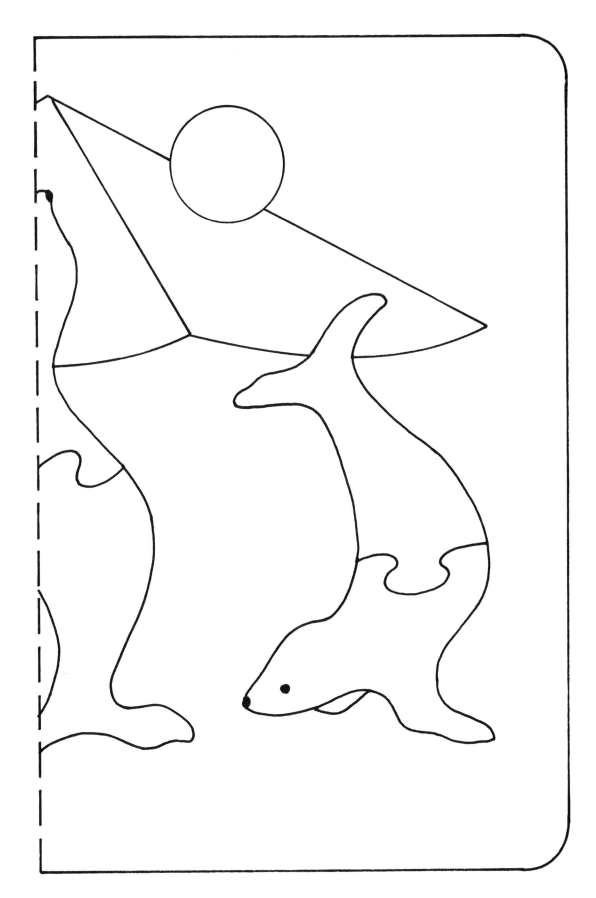

163

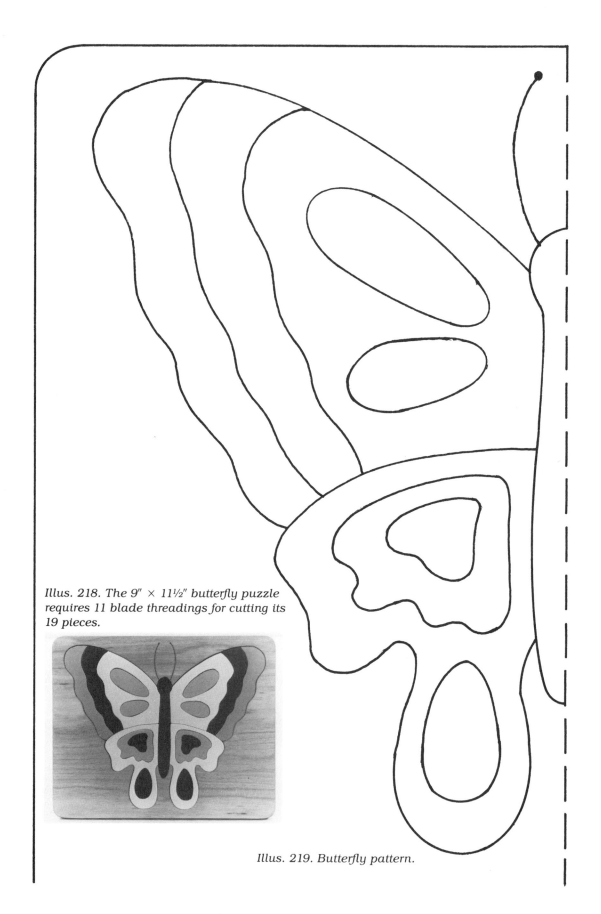

Illus. 218. The 9″ × 11½″ butterfly puzzle requires 11 blade threadings for cutting its 19 pieces.

Illus. 219. Butterfly pattern.

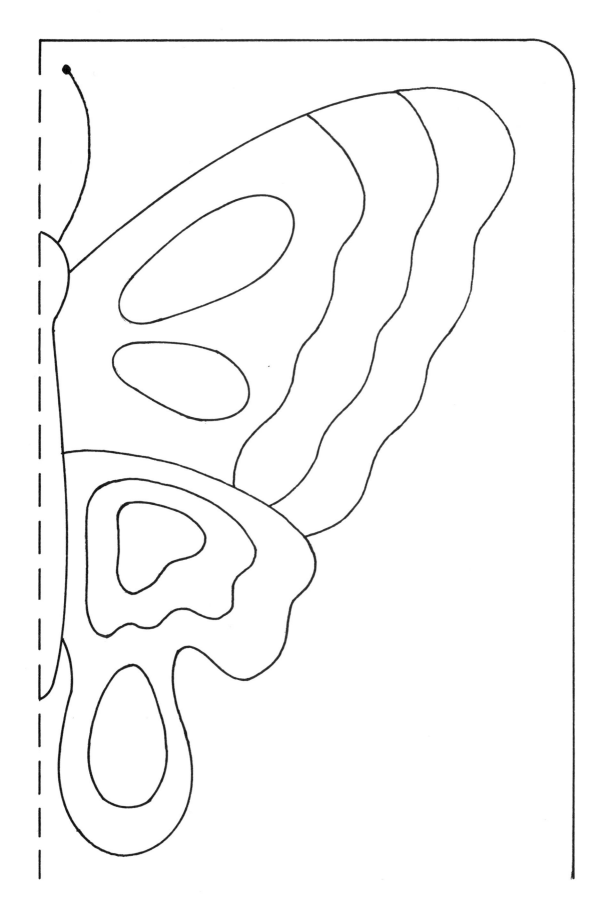

165

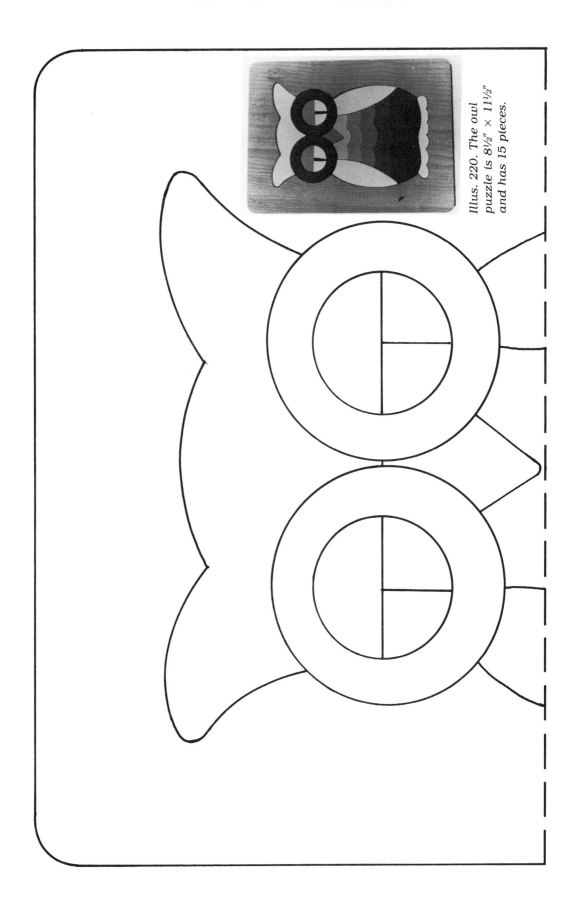

Illus. 220. The owl puzzle is 8½" × 11½" and has 15 pieces.

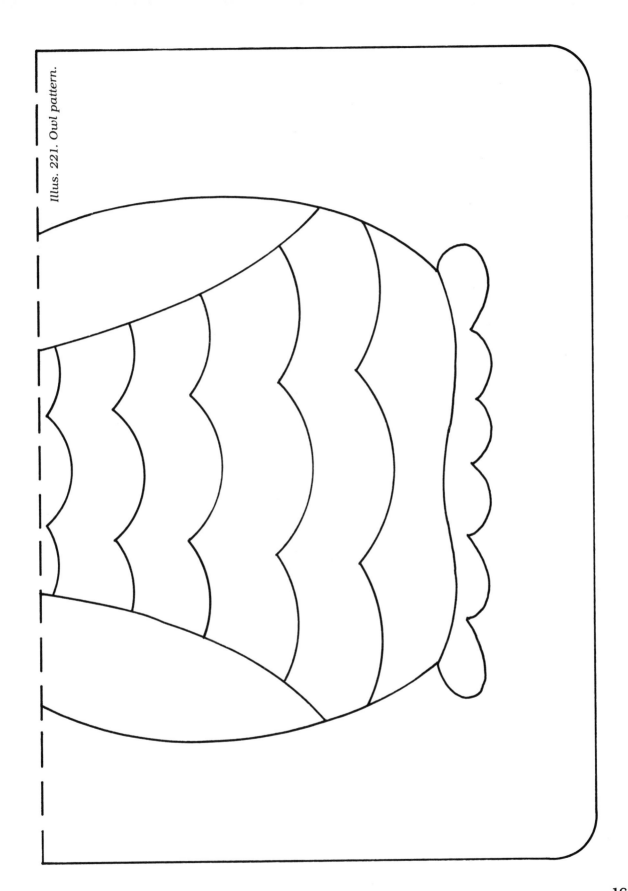

Illus. 221. Owl pattern.

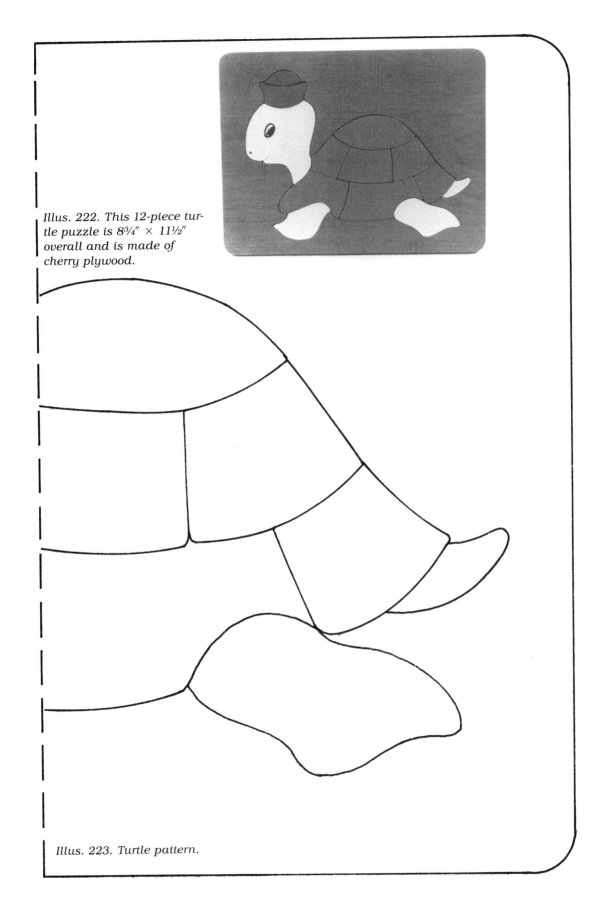

Illus. 222. This 12-piece turtle puzzle is 8¾″ × 11½″ overall and is made of cherry plywood.

Illus. 223. Turtle pattern.

Illus. 224. The snail puzzle has 13 pieces and is cut from 9½″ × 12″ teak plywood.

Illus. 225. Snail pattern.

Illus. 226. The dove puzzle is 7½" × 10" and has just seven pieces. (Turn to pages 174 and 175 for the pattern.)

Illus. 227. This cute whale puzzle has 19 pieces and is 8¾" × 12". (Turn to pages 176 and 177 for the pattern.)

Illus. 228. The dove and whale patterns were layered to make this double puzzle. Three layers of ¼"-thick plywood, including the one backing layer, were used.

Illus. 229. Dove pattern.

175

Illus. 230. Whale pattern.

176

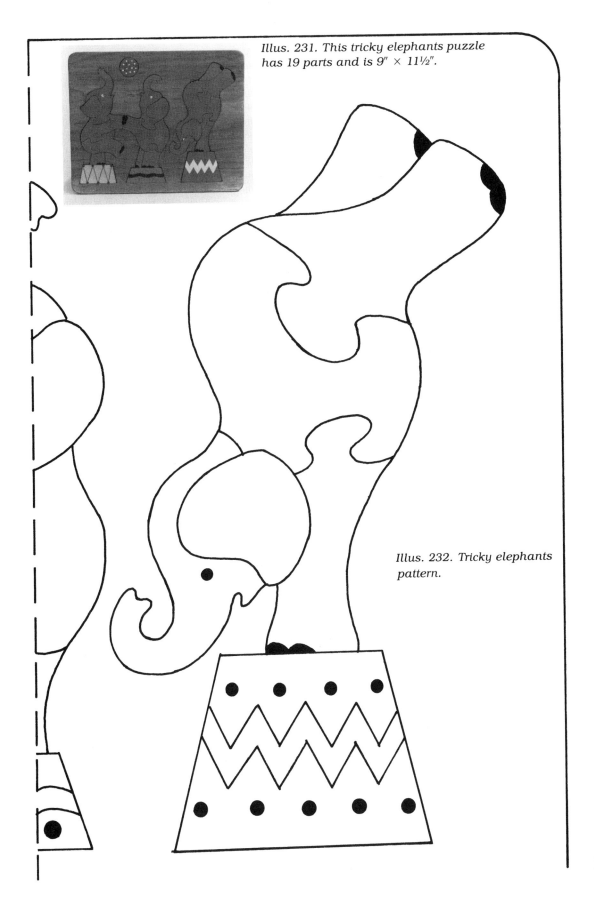

Illus. 231. This tricky elephants puzzle has 19 parts and is 9″ × 11½″.

Illus. 232. Tricky elephants pattern.

Illus. 233. The bear family puzzle is 8½″ × 10½″ and has 12 pieces. (Turn to pages 182 and 183 for the pattern.)

Illus. 234. The air balloon puzzle with optional personalization has 13 pieces and is 9″ wide by 11½″ high. (Turn to pages 184 and 185 for the air balloon pattern and to page 186 for the alphabet pattern.)

Illus. 235. Pattern for the bear family puzzle.

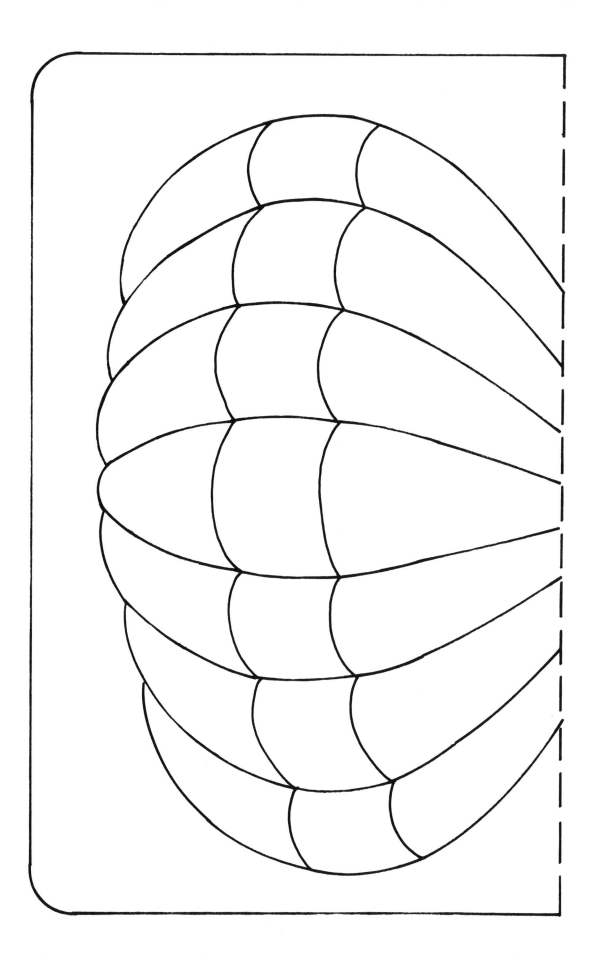

Illus. 236. Air balloon pattern.

185

ABCDEFGHIJ
KLMNOPQRST
UVWXYZ

Illus. 237. Full-size alphabet pattern for personalizing the air balloon puzzle and other puzzles.

Illus. 238. The juggling clown puzzle is cut into 14 pieces and is 8½″ × 12″.

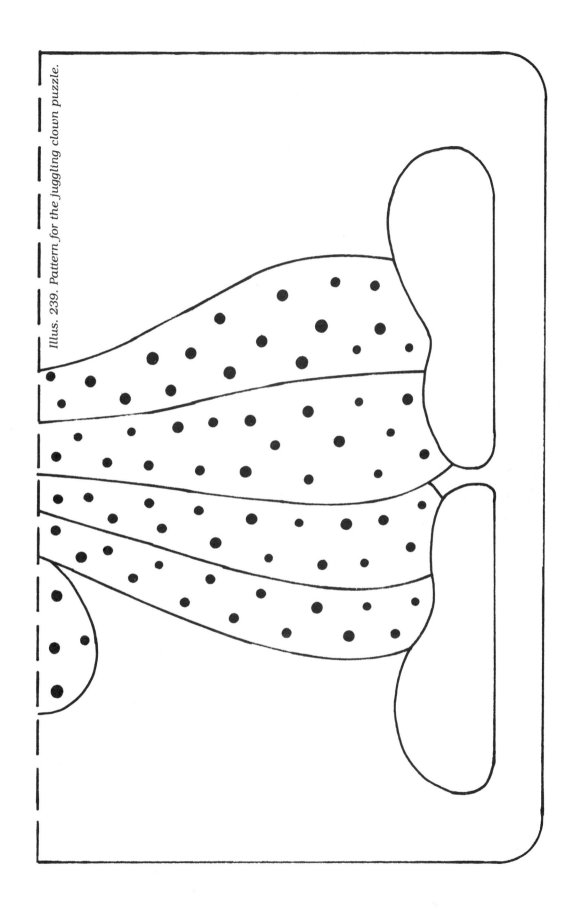

Illus. 239. Pattern for the juggling clown puzzle.

189

Illus. 240. This number puzzle measures 8¾″ × 12″. *(Turn to pages 192 and 193 for the pattern.)*

Illus. 241. This
number puzzle of
stacking blocks has
only 11 pieces and is
9″ × 12″. (Turn to
pages 194 and 195 for
the pattern.)

Illus. 242. Each num-
bered block is one
piece. The sharp cor-
ner lines are inked
with a straightedge.

Illus. 243. Number puzzle pattern.

Illus. 244. Pattern for numbered blocks puzzle.

Illus. 245. This is the classic alphabet puzzle. With the letters connected as designed, the puzzle requires only three piercing cuts; this is in contrast to 26 blade threadings if the letters are not touching each other. The overall size of the puzzle is 9½″ × 18½″.

Illus. 246. Pattern for the alphabet puzzle (continued on pages 198 and 199).

199

Illus. 247. Design your own name-and-phone-number puzzle using the patterns on the previous pages. Enlarge or reduce as desired.

Illus. 248. Here is a challenging 44-piece alphabet puzzle. It's made from two layers of ⅜" plywood that is 10½" × 12", with a ⅜" × ¾" solid wood frame glued to the edge of the bottom piece of plywood.

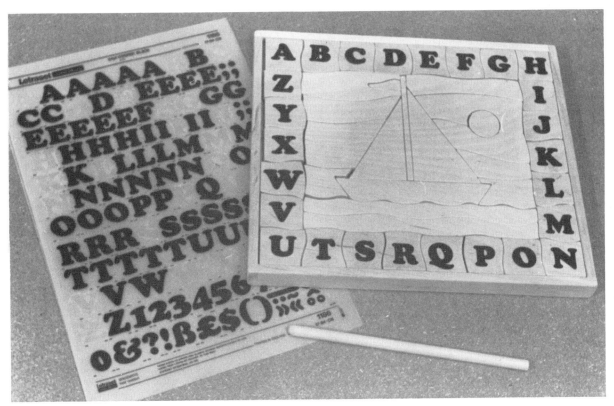

Illus. 249. Lettering art can be painted directly on the wood or achieved by using press-on type. However, the latter method may be less durable. *(Turn to pages 202–204 for the alphabet with boat pattern.)*

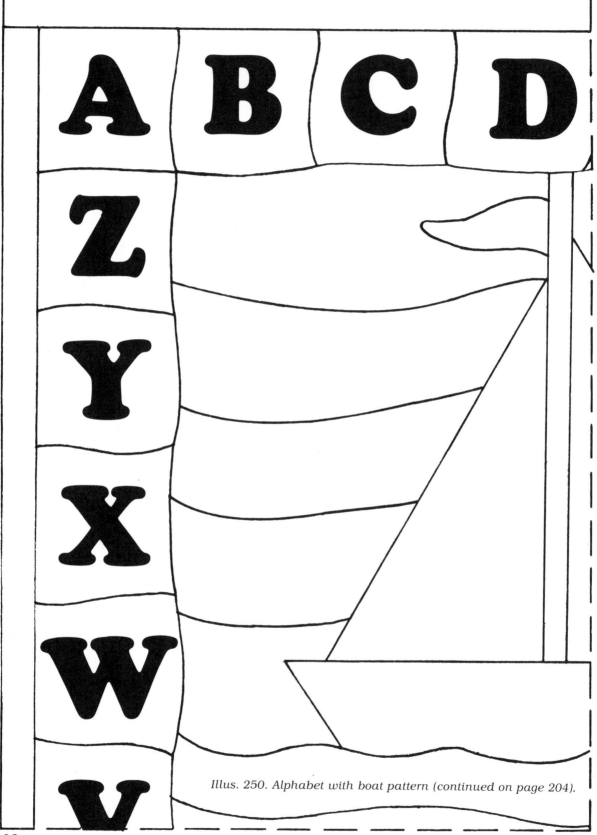

Illus. 250. Alphabet with boat pattern (continued on page 204).

E F G H

I

J

K

L

M

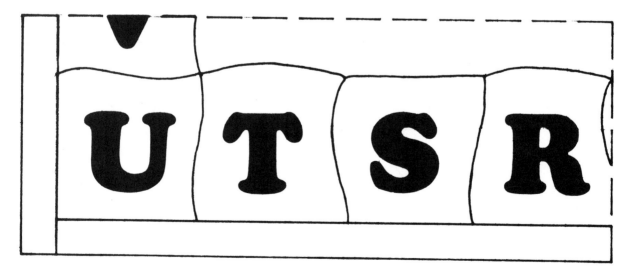

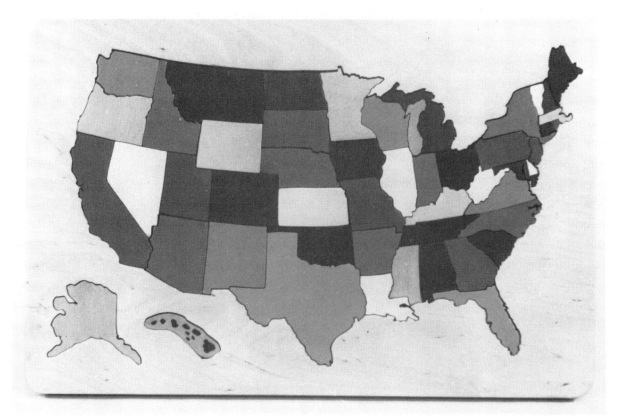

Illus. 251. This United States map puzzle requires 10″ × 15½″ plywood material. (The pattern begins on page 207.)

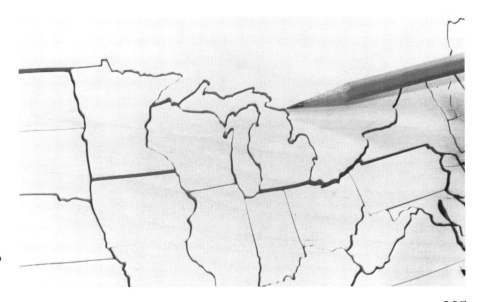

Illus. 252. Upper and lower Michigan are connected as a one-piece state. Lake Michigan can be an extra piece, or glued to the backer panel.

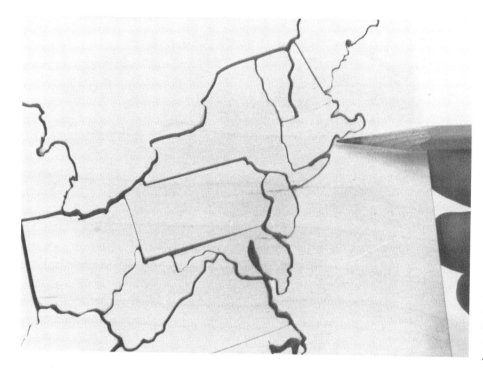

Illus. 253. Some of the small eastern states are combined to eliminate extremely small pieces.

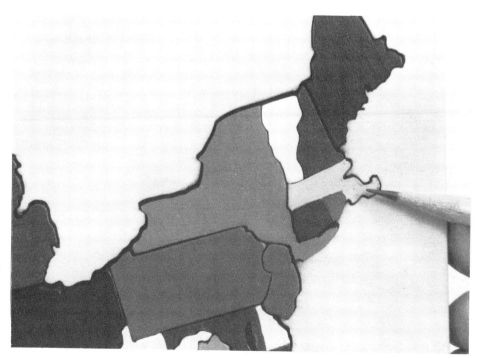

Illus. 254. Massachusetts, Connecticut, and Rhode Island are each painted a different color but sawn as just one piece. The same goes for Delaware and Maryland.

206

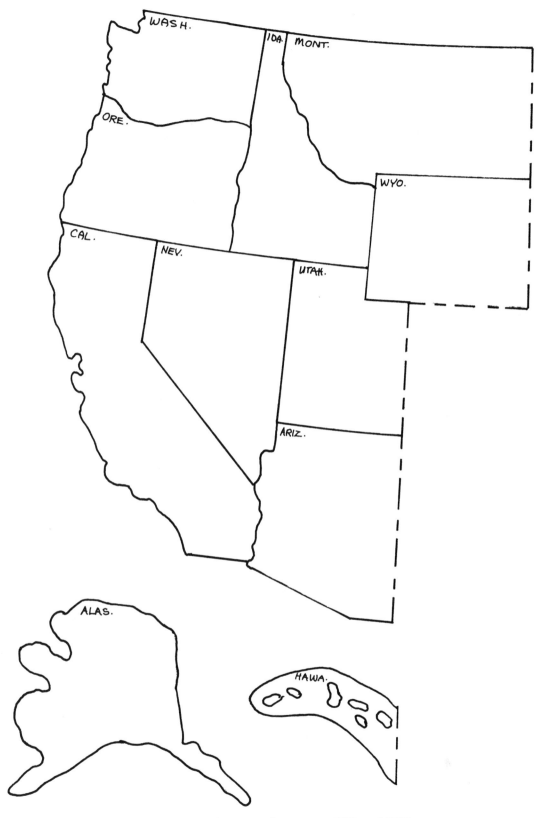

Illus. 255. United States map pattern (continued on pages 208 and 209).

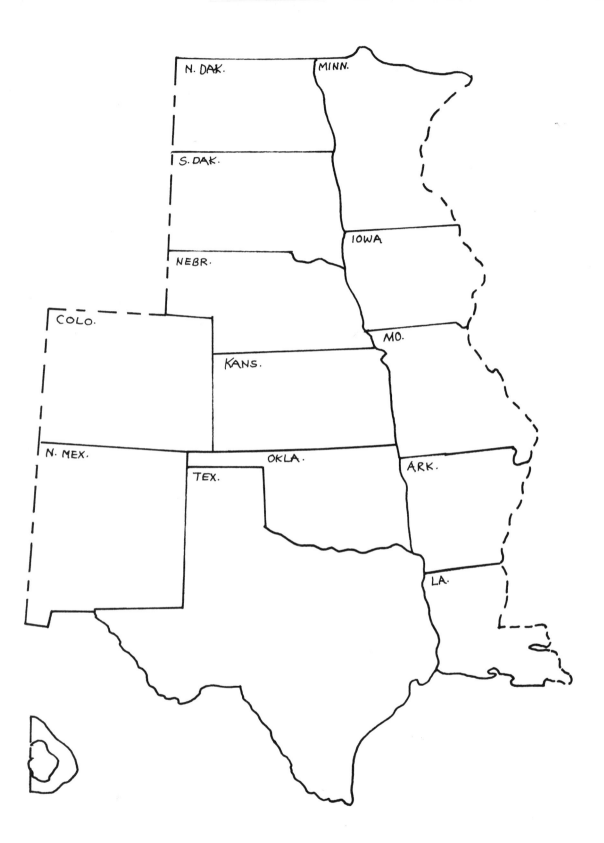

N. DAK.

MINN.

S. DAK.

NEBR.

IOWA

COLO.

KANS.

MO.

N. MEX.

OKLA.

ARK.

TEX.

LA.

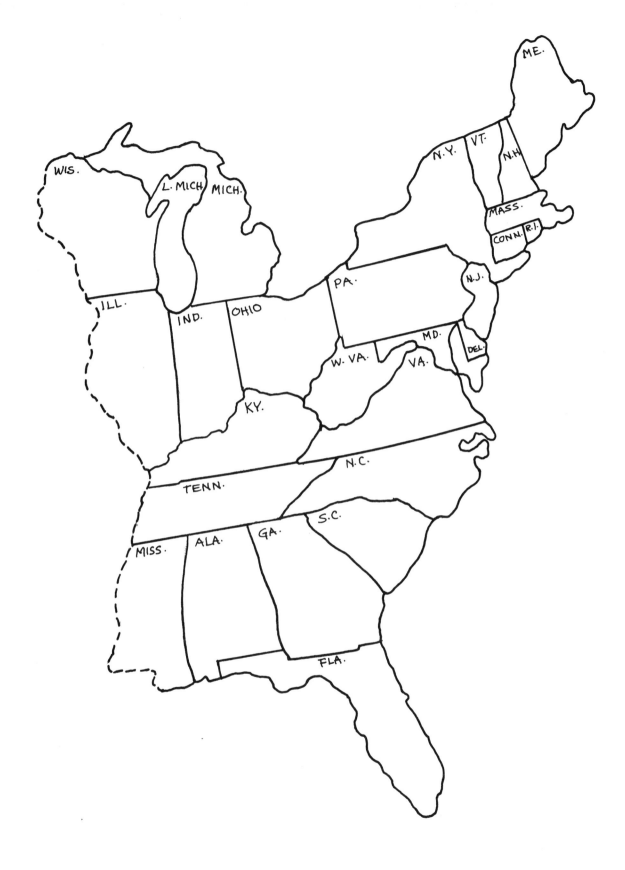

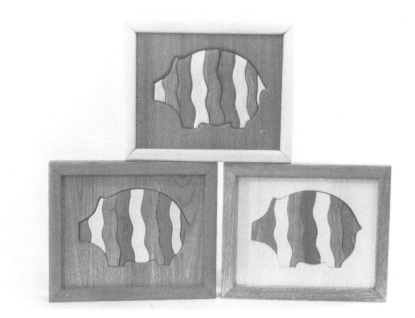

Illus. 256. These are inlay puzzles made of ½"-thick solid wood in ¾" × 1⅜" grooved frames. Each has a ⅛" hardboard backer. These puzzles were stack-sawn from different woods. Notice that the grain runs vertically. (Turn to pages 216 and 217 for the pig puzzle pattern.)

Illus. 257. Begin with three boards that are ½" thick × 9½" wide × 7¼" long, each made of a different material. Pine, redwood, and butternut were used in this example. Note the grain directions.

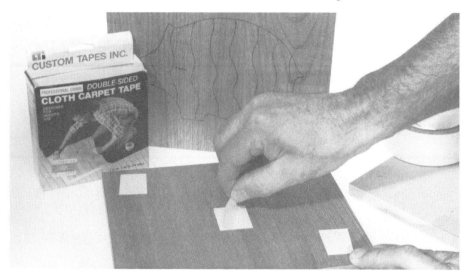

Illus. 258. Apply double-face tape to hold the layers together for stack cutting. See Illus. 265.

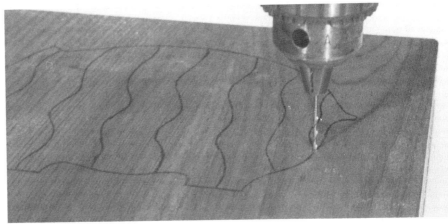

Illus. 259. Be sure that your saw's cutting capacity can handle the combined thicknesses.

Illus. 260. Drill a small hole for blade threading.

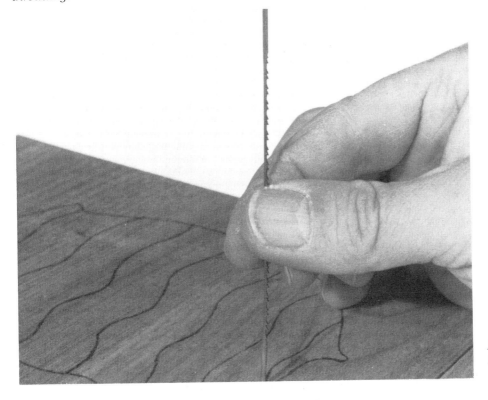

Illus. 261. Thread the blade.

211

Illus. 262. Saw around the pig profile first.

Illus. 263. With the pieces of double-sided tape strategically located, the cutout pig profile should remain intact.

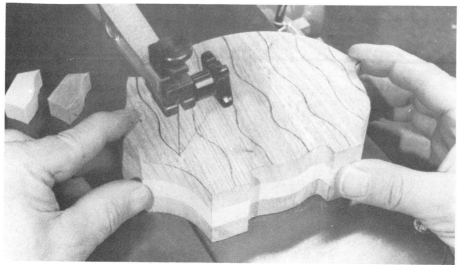

Illus. 264. When you cut the pieces, you should saw alternately from the head and tail ends.

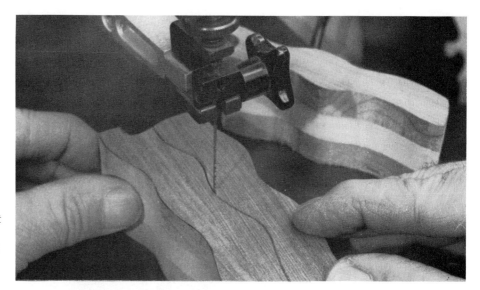

Illus. 265. The last cut will be made through the area of the central piece of double-faced tape.

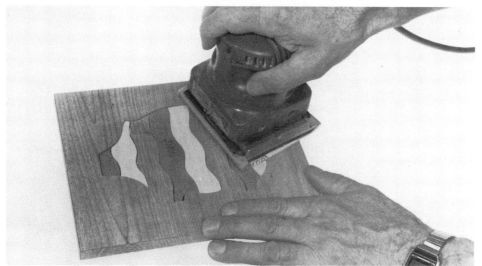

Illus. 266. Sanding the faces is shown here.

Illus. 267. Rounding over just the face edges makes the pieces one-sided and thus easier to assemble. If the edges are equally rounded or square, top and bottom, the puzzle is more challenging.

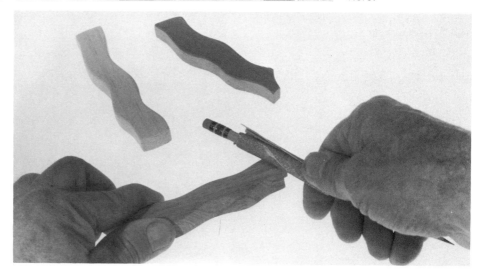

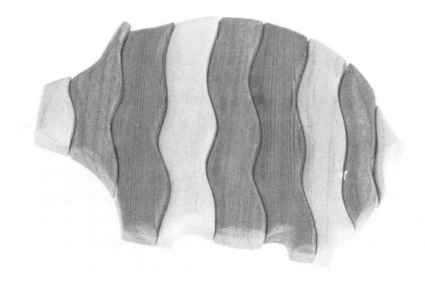

Illus. 268. The pieces of this puzzle have all the top edges rounded over.

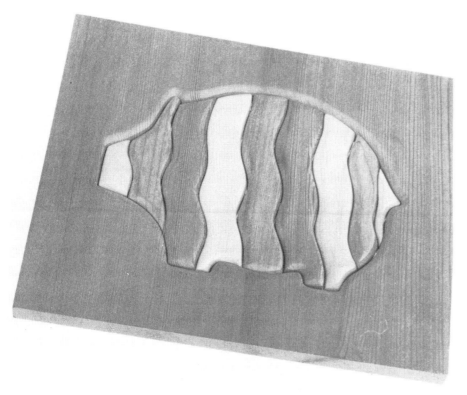

Illus. 269. Rounding the inside edges of the pig enhances the puzzle.

214

Illus. 270. These are all the puzzle pieces. Note that the ⅛″ hardboard backer is cut the same size as the piece to be framed.

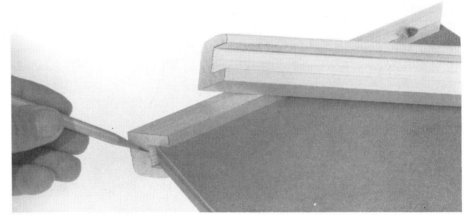

Illus. 271. A clearance is provided to allow for expansion of the wood within the frame. See the section drawing on the pattern.

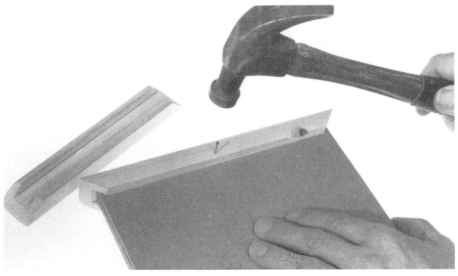

Illus. 272. After all pieces have been finished (in this example, with Danish oil), only one nail driven into the upper frame member will center the panel to the space within the frame.

215

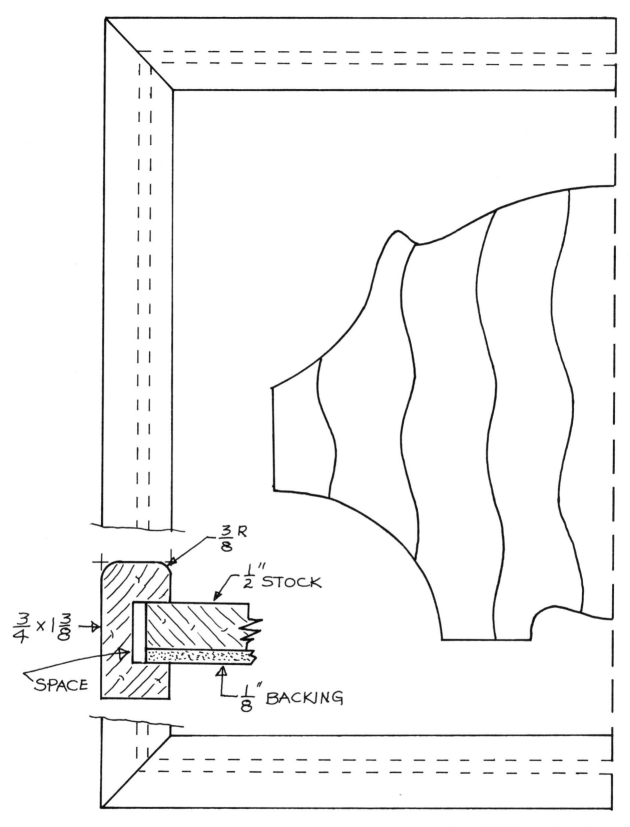

$\frac{3}{8}$ R

$\frac{1}{2}$" STOCK

$\frac{3}{4} \times 1\frac{3}{8}$

SPACE

$\frac{1}{8}$" BACKING

Illus. 273. Pig puzzle pattern.

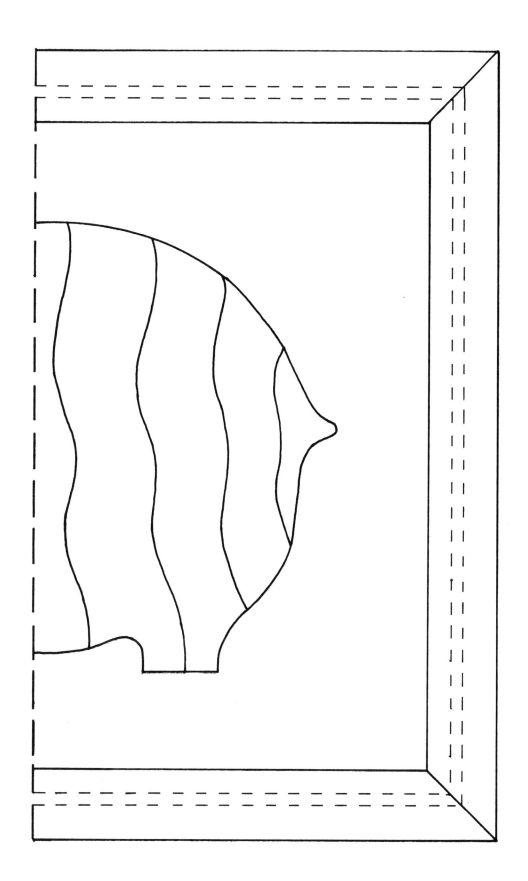

7

Some Tricky Ideas

This chapter offers a few novel puzzle patterns and some ideas that are somewhat of a departure from the previously discussed puzzle-making techniques. For example, the six- or nine-piece jigsaw puzzle made from a little postage stamp is more of an exercise in technique than an effort to create a useful puzzle. The fun lies mostly in the doing; its best use is as a conversation piece. You must have excellent eyesight and a steady hand to make this minipuzzle. If you are up to the challenge, Illus. 274–278 will assist you through the steps.

Interlocking puzzles made from a turned fat dowel and a puzzle sawn from a flat disc of plywood are two other interesting ideas (Illus. 279). It's easier to cut the dowel puzzle with a band saw, but a good scroll saw can also do the job. Make your dowel a little longer than needed. This will give you some extra material to hold on to and will allow you to make one or two trial cuts. The technique is a little tricky, but you'll soon get the hang of it. See Illus. 280–283 for the patterns and some helpful photos.

If you take any scrap piece of sheet stock or a block of solid wood and cut it into pieces with wavy or irregular edges, you

Illus. 274 (left). Here is a six-piece puzzle made from a postage stamp. Illus. 275 (right). Adhere the stamp to some thin three-ply 3-mm (⅛″) Baltic birch plywood and then divide it into sections with light pencil lines.

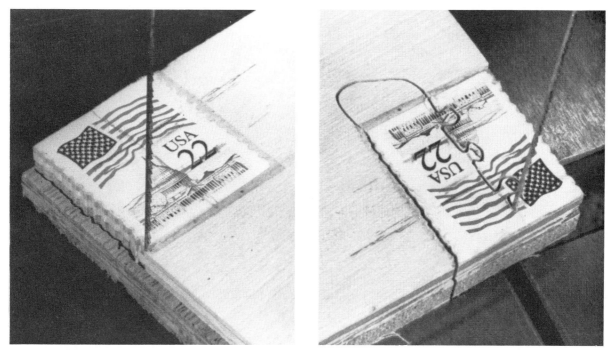

Illus. 276 (left). Use double-face tape to secure the thin plywood to a thicker backing. Cut along one edge, following the perforations on the edge of the stamp. Illus. 277 (right). Cut the second perforated edge and then swing back, making a vertical cut up the middle of the stamp, as shown.

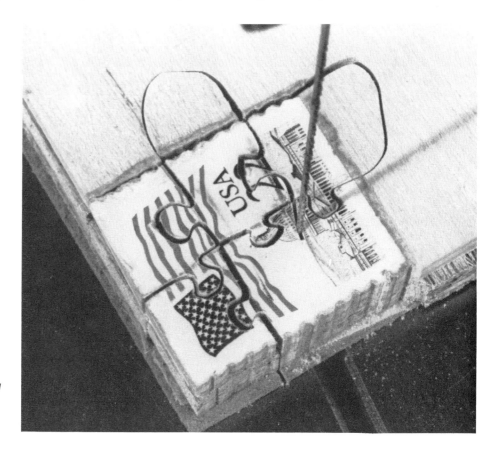

Illus. 278. Make the crosswise separating cuts, as shown, to complete the tiny puzzle.

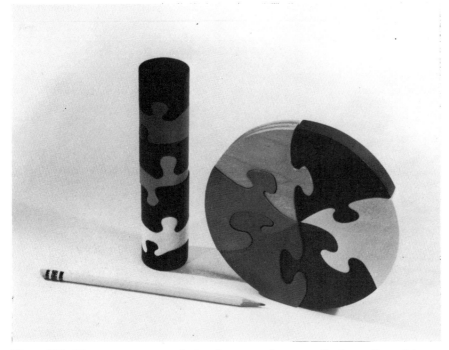

Illus. 279. These two unusual stand-up puzzles were first mentioned in Chapter 5.

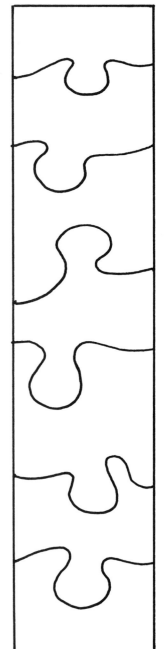

Illus. 280. A 1½"-diameter dowel that is 6¾" long is used for this interesting and decorative puzzle. Rotate each interlocking cut-line pattern approximately 10° to 20° so that they are slightly offset to the adjoining piece. You can employ this puzzle concept to make puzzles of any length and in a diameter up to that of the thickness-cutting capacity of your scroll saw.

Illus. 281. This 1½"-diameter dowel can be cut on this scroll saw with the aid of the triangular block-supporting fixture.

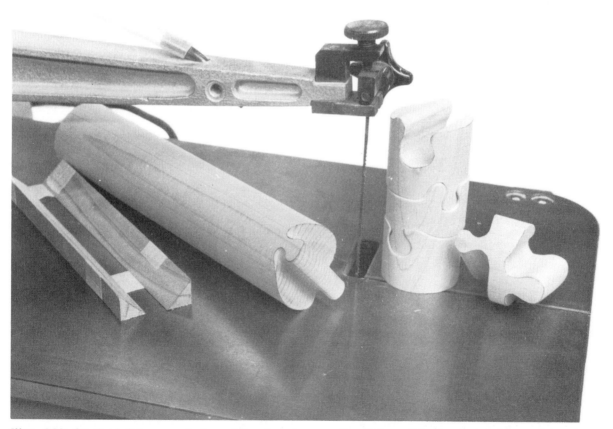

Illus. 282. On the left is a good view of the dowel-supporting fixture. It is simply two triangular strips of wood and some filament tape. Note the completed cuts.

Illus. 283. Here is the pattern for the disc puzzle. This one was made 6″ in diameter and sawn from ¾″ hardwood plywood. Similar puzzles but of other diameters and material thicknesses with any number of pieces can be developed as desired.

can make a quick, interesting, and challenging puzzle. A two-dimensional example cut from a scrap of sheet plastic is shown in Illus. 284–287. A puzzle employ-

Illus. 285. In this photo the plastic puzzle is nearly assembled. The same puzzle could be sawn from plywood or any other suitable sheet material.

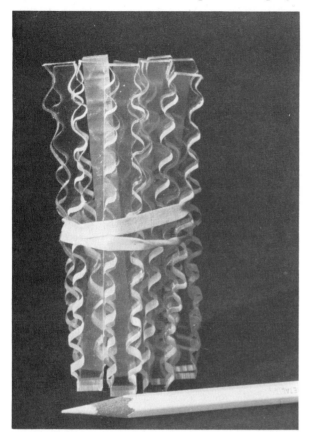

Illus. 284. Irregularly cut strips of clear plastic that look almost identical and are held together with a rubber band make a challenging puzzle package. The objective is to fit the pieces together to make a flat rectangular shape.

ing the same idea but composed of three-dimensional irregular pieces is depicted in Illus. 288–291.

Most of the preceding puzzles can be made to any size that is within the stock-cutting capacities of your scroll saw. In fact, to make these puzzles, you really don't need exact patterns, although some general guidelines may be helpful. By and large, the average scroll sawer should be able to saw this sort of work freehand at will.

The last two patterns in the book are

some tricky square puzzles with straight-edged pieces. Both making and "playing" these puzzles is a little trickier than one might expect. Illus. 292–296 depict these puzzles and show some tips for making them. The most important requirement is that you start with pieces that are perfectly square. Thus, the blank starting pieces should be accurately sawn on a table saw, if one is available. Otherwise, you must be

Illus. 286. Each piece is sawn freehand by cutting back and forth across the guidelines marked on the plastic's protective masking, as shown.

absolutely sure that you scroll-saw very precisely on the pattern lines given.

The puzzle ideas discussed and illustrated in this chapter are also intended to motivate you towards experimenting with a variety of unusual materials and exploring the potential of sawing out designs in uncommon shapes and sizes. Once you do, you'll be well on your way towards making some very creative puzzles.

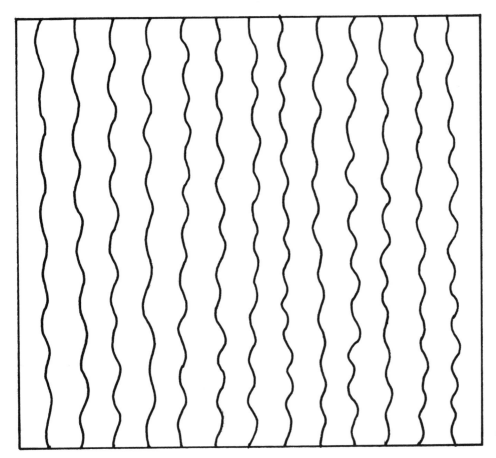

Illus. 287. Here is a pattern, should you want one.

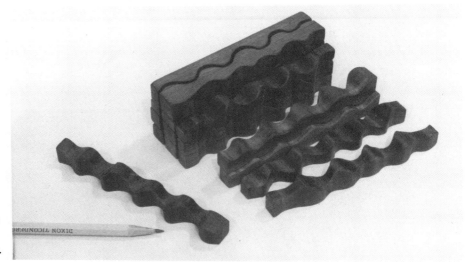

Illus. 288. This is a 16-piece puzzle made from a 1¾" square of walnut that is 5" long.

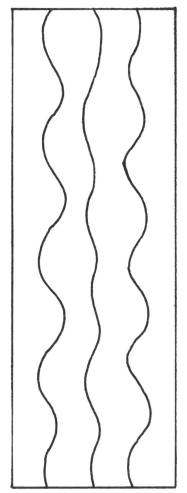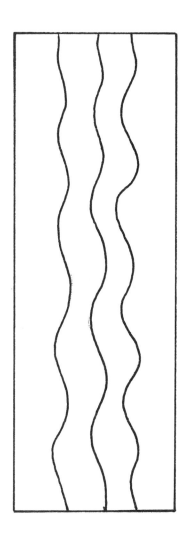

Illus. 289. Here are the patterns for the 16-piece block puzzle. Cutting is done on two adjoining surfaces of the block, which results in three-dimensional, contoured puzzle pieces.

Illus. 290. This photo shows the first three irregular ripping cuts completed.

225

Illus. 291. With the four pieces taped back together, the second series of cuts is made from the adjoining side. Make the two outside cuts before doing the last cut down the middle.

Illus. 292. Here are two seemingly very simple puzzles that might surprise even the brightest puzzler. Each puzzle is made from two perfect 6″ × 6″ squares of ⅜″-thick plywood.

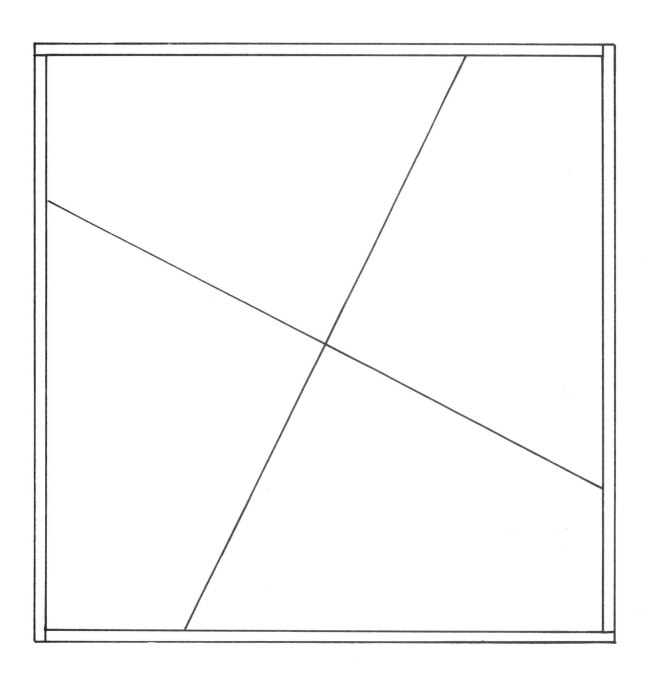

Illus. 293. This is square puzzle pattern No. 1. All four puzzle pieces are identical. Solid wood strips that are ⅛″ × ½″ × 6⅛″ are glued to the base to contain the pieces.

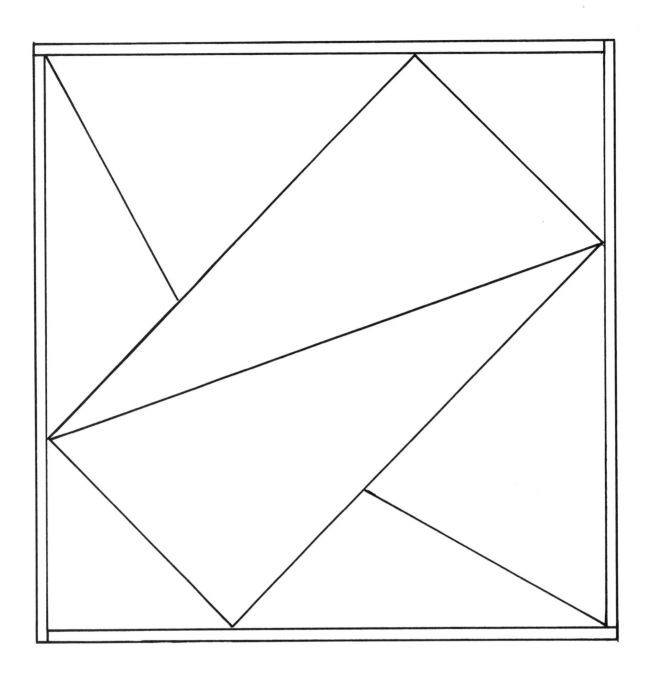

Illus. 294. This is square puzzle pattern No. 2. Notice that this puzzle has four pairs of identical pieces, which dictates doing some very careful and precise saw work.

Illus. 295. Using a wide blade makes cutting straight lines easier. Cut directly, centering on each line. This puzzle is being cut from ⅜″ Baltic birch plywood.

Illus. 296. Here is a simple way of clamping the glued-on strips of ⅛″ × ½″ × 6⅛″ wood to the base piece of ⅜″ plywood.

8

Finishing and Painting Techniques

Puzzles can be finished in a wide variety of different ways. The possibilities range from no finish at all to natural oils; varnishes; stock wood dye colors; and specially mixed stains, paints, and enamels. You can also use a combination of different finishes on just one puzzle. Natural finishes coupled with bright colors is one typical example.

We certainly do not advocate any one brand of finish or specific method as being the final word on the subject of finishing puzzles. There are not only many different products available for puzzle finishing, but many techniques not covered here that are well worth considering. If you are an experienced woodworker, you may already have established certain finishing

Illus. 297. Check all labels to be sure that all coating materials are lead-free and non-toxic. Although this brand is popular for finishing metal surfaces, we have found it to be one of the most durable color-pigmented finishes available for wood.

systems that give you the results you want. We are not suggesting that you change them.

One key point, however, that all parents and customers insist upon is that puzzles be finished with nontoxic coatings (Illus. 297). Of course, one way to be absolutely safe is not to apply any finish whatsoever to the wood. Many of the stand-up puzzles sold today come without any finish, even though children tend to prefer puzzles in bright color combinations. There is something about older-looking, well-used works of unfinished wood that is appealing to adults, but children don't typically share this fascination. See Illus. 298 and 299.

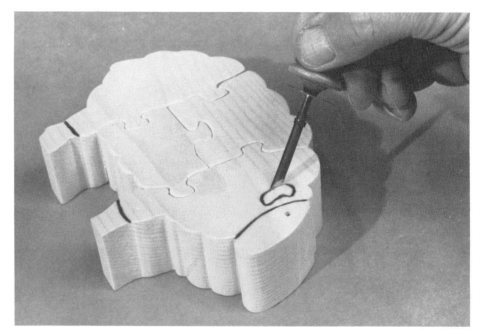

Illus. 298. A wood-burning tool can be used to give detail and color to unfinished wood. This puzzle can be left unfinished or coated with natural oils or a satin varnish.

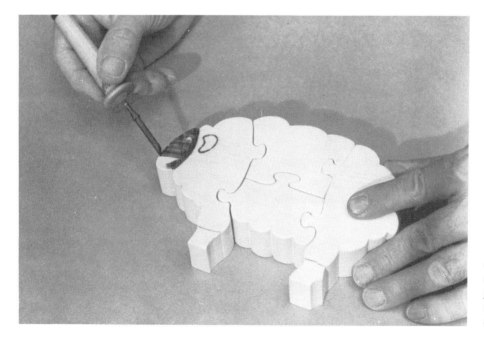

Illus. 299. This photo shows using the flat part of a woodburning tool to highlight an area.

Natural finishes do accentuate and enrich the grain pattern, or figure, of the wood. Vegetable and mineral oils are very safe and they are readily available and easy to apply. See Illus. 300 and 301. A good choice is peanut oil.

Illus. 300. Applying a natural oil finish to pine stand-up puzzles is shown here. A foam-sponge brush is used as the applicator.

Illus. 301. Some finishing tools include the larger foam brushes, a pallet knife, and finer bristle brushes for detailing.

A commercial product that we often recommend and use ourselves is Watco Danish Oil. This is a blend of resins and oils that penetrates deeply into the cellular structure of the wood. It reacts chemically with natural substances of the wood, curing by polymerization, which has a hardening effect on the wood. One publicly funded testing agency unofficially stated that the surface hardness of some woods can be increased by as much as 25 percent with this product. This is especially beneficial when you're using softwoods and if your puzzles will be put to rugged use. It's important to know that the full polymerization curing process of the Watco oils takes about 30 days. This time span is needed before the finish can be regarded as nontoxic. Available in a wide selection of pigmented colors, Watco Danish Oil finishes (Illus. 302) permit staining and finishing, all in one easy operation. To apply these finishes, you simply flood the surfaces to the point of refusal and then wipe away all of the excess. You can buy Watco Danish Oil products at local paint and hardware outlets or at building and woodworking centers. We finished all of the backgrounds and backers of the inlay puzzles in this book with Watco's Natural Danish Oil.

Most varnishes and epoxies, once ap-

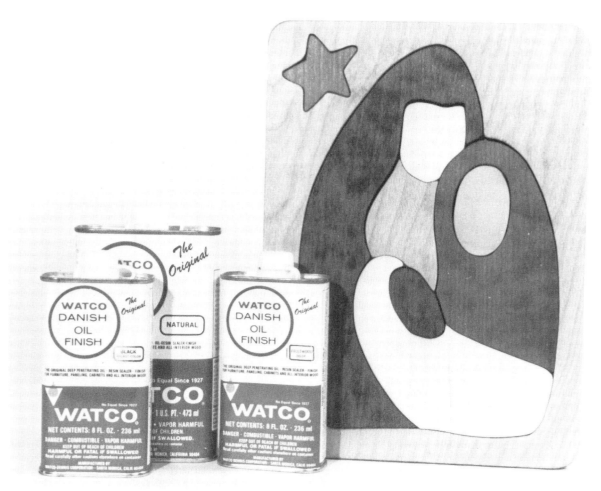

Illus. 302. Natural and pigmented oil finishes can provide a variety of colors or special emphasis to individual pieces within the same puzzle.

plied and cured, are also nontoxic. We seldom use varnishes of any type, except where we want a good surface with a natural finish to be a base for fine-line detailing. Lines from permanent markers and fine pens will bleed when applied to the surfaces of unfinished wood. Raw wood is just like an ink blotter. See Illus. 303.

In cases where we want to make fine-line detailing with pen and ink or a permanent marker, we first varnish the puzzle with quick-drying spray urethane and sand it lightly with a fine abrasive. Then we do the detailing, and when that's dry, we spray a protective mist of urethane varnish over it again. Once that dries, the puzzle can be given another, heavier protective top coat.

Although the handy aerosol sprays tend to be too expensive for commercial operations, they do make finishing quick and convenient. See Illus. 304, 305, and 306. Plan to finish all pieces of the same color, stain, or whatever at the same time. This saves time. A dowel with a pointed nail or needles driven into the end makes a good holder for spray finishing. The marks it leaves are too inconspicuous to be concerned about—especially if they are in the edge, rather than the surface, of the puzzle piece. When you use the dowel holder, you can also paint both sides at the same time. A light mist sprayed to the inside edges is all that's needed for stand-up puzzles. The outside edges need to be finished (painted) the same way as the other visible face surfaces.

Latex and acrylic paints are water-soluble and nontoxic. See Illus. 307. They are easy to use, and you can mix them yourself to get just the right color. Or, if you'd pre-

Illus. 303. The letter "E" on the right is a good example of bleeding. Most pens and markers will bleed this way when applied to raw or improperly finished wood, and certain inks will bleed when another top coat is applied over them. Always make a trial test. Permanent markers are preferred for most jobs.

234

Illus. 304. Various products typically bought at a hardware dealer's are satisfactory for nonproduction puzzle finishing.

fer, you can purchase practically any color you wish from a paint store with a custom-mixing service. Solid, or opaque, colors can be used to hide a range of sins (de-fects). Cracks, dents, pores, and the like can be hidden if they are properly filled prior to painting. See Illus. 308.

It's recommended to use primers with

Illus. 305. It's difficult to hold stand-up puzzle pieces and spray them with enamels on all sur-faces at the same time. Use a dowel with needles set into the end to solve this problem.

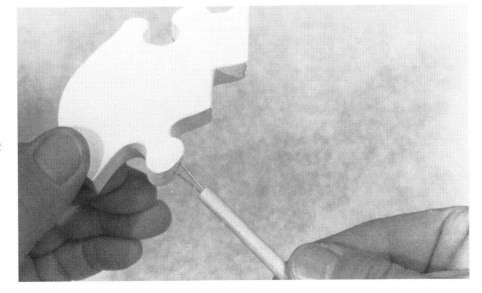

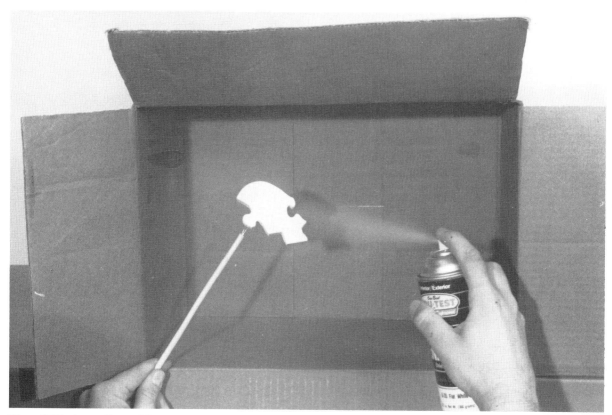

Illus. 306. A cardboard box makes a short-term spray booth. Caution: Be sure adequate ventilation is provided.

Illus. 307. Latex and acrylic paints are water-soluble, easy to use, nontoxic, and available in any color you want if you don't wish to mix your own.

Illus. 308. Any one of the various wood fillers available should be used to fill in voids and similar defects before painting. Edges of cheap plywoods especially need attention.

certain paints and enamels. They do a lot to help hide, or cover up, many defects as well as certain aspects of the wood itself, such as the undesirable wild grain of Douglas fir or yellow pine plywood. Remember to sand dry primers before applying the top coat. See Illus. 309 to 312.

Sometimes you may not want to hide the grain or other characteristics of the wood. With some experimentation, you may find that pigmented finishes applied directly from the can without any previously applied primers or sealers will produce very interesting results.

Another way to allow the grain figure of the wood to show through is by using nontoxic water-soluble wood dyes and stains, which are available in a good selection of very brilliant colors. See Illus. 313. These

products work best on the lighter woods, such as pine, poplar, cedar, basswood, and soft maple. The Swedish wood dyes and aniline stains come in a powder that is dissolved in water (or alcohol). All kinds of bright colors are available, including red, yellow, orange, green, blue, and brown. Several of the large, colorful stand-up puzzles in the color section of this book, such as the apple, pear, and duck, were finished with these dry-powdered dyes and stains. If these products are not available locally, you can obtain them from Klockit Company in Lake Geneva, Wisconsin. Some of these products raise the grain fibres, but certain steps can be taken to alleviate this problem. For instance, you can sponge off the wood first with water, and then, after it dries, sand the surfaces

Illus. 309. Fine-grit sanding (lightly) after priming and between top coats makes the ultimate top coat much smoother. This all takes time, however.

Illus. 310. With a foam-sponge brush, you can apply some finishes quickly and very smoothly.

238

Illus. 311. This photo shows making a pencil guideline for detailing.

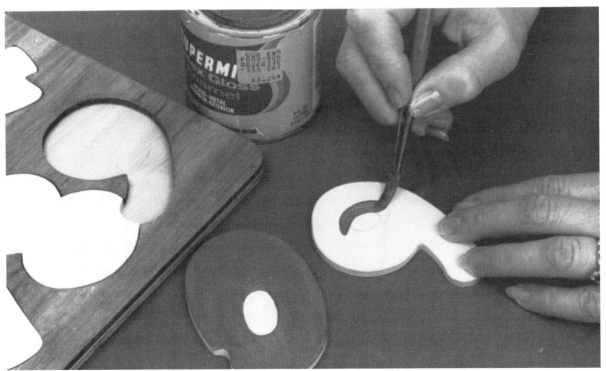

Illus. 312. Sometimes it's easier to use a fairly well-loaded brush to work the coating material to the line.

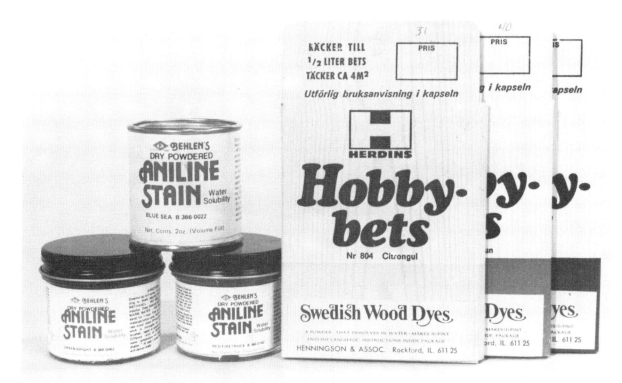

Illus. 313. Aniline stains and wood dyes are powdered and water-soluble, and can be used to give bright, brilliant colors to wood without hiding the grain.

Illus. 314. You can create eye details simply by using permanent markers, ink pens, and paint. And you can indicate a nose just by employing a small line or a touch of paint.

with fine sandpaper. Then you can apply the stain or dye, and after that, use a top coat of a sealer or varnish.

Of course, many different kinds and brands of finishing products are available for staining and varnishing. We suggest that you consult your local paint dealer for products that he may recommend.

In addition to finishing, certain easy-to-do but fundamental detailing techniques can add significantly to the artistic quality and professional look of your puzzles. Illus. 314 shows various examples of de-tailed eyes that were created with perma-nent markers, ink pens, and paint. Also, in Illus. 314, notice how a simple line or mark can be used to indicate a nose. With the Raggy Ann inlay puzzle in Illus. 315, you can see how the little extra details—such as the folds in the bow and sleeve, the uniformly sized dots in the skirt, and the heart-shaped mouth—can add a lot of interest to a puzzle.

We've found that acrylic paints work es-pecially well for painting details. They are easy to thin with water to achieve just the

Illus. 315. This Raggy Ann inlay puzzle is a good example of how various easy-to-do de-tailing techniques can add a lot of interest to a puzzle.

right consistency, and you can mix whatever color you might want.

Illus. 316, 317, and 318 show how effective painting a simple fine line can be. Dots, shown in Illus. 319–322, are fun, quick, and easy to make, and they have

Illus. 316. Here, a short, tapered paint stroke simulates a fold in the fabric.

Illus. 317. Here, a painted line is used to show separation.

242

Illus. 318. Painting the bow is shown here. Note how the line width tapers, which is achieved by a lifting stroke.

Illus. 319. You can make dots with the handle end of your brush dipped in paint.

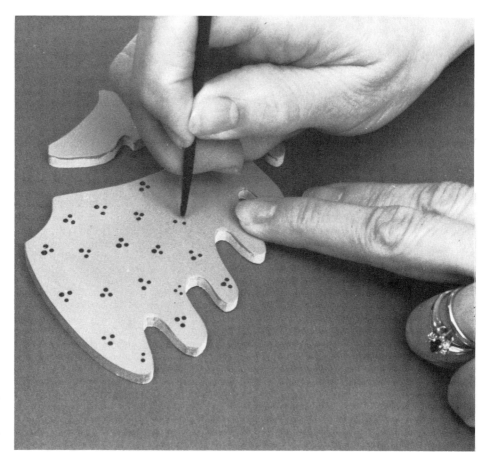

Illus. 320. A series of three dots creates a decorative pattern on the dress.

Illus. 321. Dots in a line are used to accentuate painted separations.

244

Illus. 322. This photo shows how you can make hearts using an artist's brush handle dipped in paint. Note the disposable palette pad being used for practice.

Illus. 323. Start the heart by making two dots next to each other. Of course, you can use larger brush handles to make larger hearts.

many applications for the creative puzzle painter. Rather than painting dots with the bristle end of the brush, simply dip the pointed handle end of your artist's brush into the paint and proceed in making the dots just as you would use your pencil to dot the letter *i*. Use different-size brush handles to make different-size dots. Do not allow dried paint to build up on the end of your brush if you want all the dots to be of uniform sizes.

Painting small hearts—individually, in a series, or in a row—can be another effective detailing technique just like making dots. See the heart-shaped mouth on the Raggy Ann puzzle in Illus. 315. To create a heart, make two dots equal in size next to each other with the end of your artist's brush handle. Then bring the two dots together, using the handle end of your brush to pull the paint to a point. See Illus. 322–326.

Finally, since signing and dating works of art can add to their value, if you're in the puzzle-making business you might want to consider stickers or a brand, giving your address or other information (Illus. 327). Stickers can be removed, but a brand is forever.

Illus. 324. Then pull paint from both dots to form the point of the heart. (Note the different-size brush handles.)

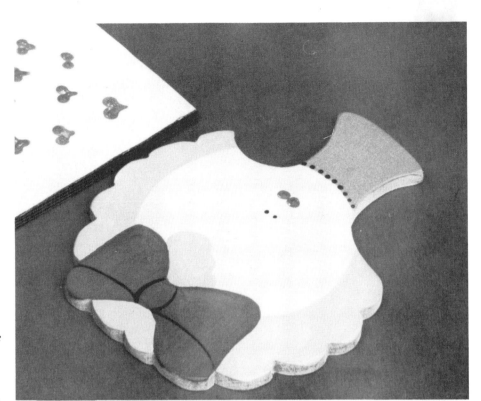

Illus. 325. Making the heart-shaped mouth on the Raggy Ann puzzle begins with two dots side by side.

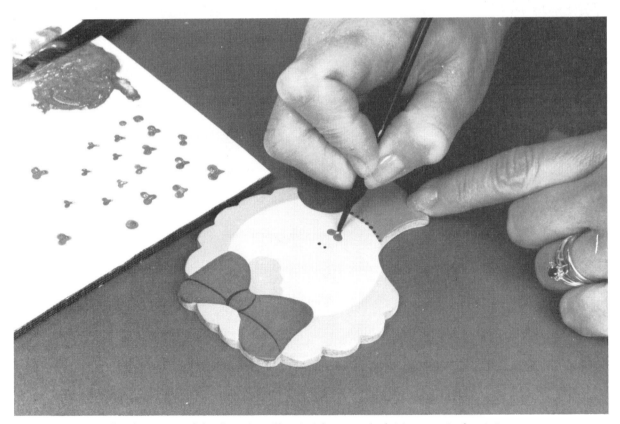

Illus. 326. To make the point of the heart, pull paint from each dot to a central point.

Illus. 327. It's a good idea to identify your work with a brand, sticker, or signature—especially if you're in the puzzle-making business.

METRIC EQUIVALENCY CHART

mm—millimetres **cm—centimetres**

INCHES TO MILLIMETRES AND CENTIMETRES

inches	mm	cm	inches	cm	inches	cm
⅛	3	0.3	9	22.9	30	76.2
¼	6	0.6	10	25.4	31	78.7
⅜	10	1.0	11	27.9	32	81.3
½	13	1.3	12	30.5	33	83.8
⅝	16	1.6	13	33.0	34	86.4
¾	19	1.9	14	35.6	35	88.9
⅞	22	2.2	15	38.1	36	91.4
1	25	2.5	16	40.6	37	94.0
1¼	32	3.2	17	43.2	38	96.5
1½	38	3.8	18	45.7	39	99.1
1¾	44	4.4	19	48.3	40	101.6
2	51	5.1	20	50.8	41	104.1
2½	64	6.4	21	53.3	42	106.7
3	76	7.6	22	55.9	43	109.2
3½	89	8.9	23	58.4	44	111.8
4	102	10.2	24	61.0	45	114.3
4½	114	11.4	25	63.5	46	116.8
5	127	12.7	26	66.0	47	119.4
6	152	15.2	27	68.6	48	121.9
7	178	17.8	28	71.1	49	124.5
8	203	20.3	29	73.7	50	127.0

About the Authors

Patrick Spielman's love of wood began when, as a child, he transformed fruit crates into toys. Now this prolific and innovative woodworker is respected worldwide as a teacher and author.

His most famous contribution to the woodworking field has been his perfection of a method to season green wood with polyethylene glycol 1000 (PEG). He went on to invent, manufacture, and distribute the PEG-Thermovat chemical seasoning system.

During his many years as shop instructor in Wisconsin, Spielman published manuals, teaching guides, and more than 14 popular books, including *Modern Wood Technology*, a college text. He also wrote six educational series on wood technology, tool use, processing techniques, design, and wood-product planning.

Author of the best-selling *Router Handbook* (over 600,000 copies sold), Spielman has served as editorial consultant to a professional magazine, and his products, techniques, and many books have been featured in numerous periodicals.

This pioneer of new ideas and inventor of countless jigs, fixtures, and designs used throughout the world is a unique combination of expert woodworker and brilliant teacher—all of which have endeared him to his many readers and to his publisher.

At Spielmans Wood Works in the woods of northern Door County, Wisconsin, he and his family create and sell some of the most durable and popular furniture products and designs available.

As both a buyer of wood products and the creator of Spielmans Wood Works Gift Shop and Gallery, Patricia Spielman ("Mrs. Pat") plays an invaluable part in the success of Spielmans Wood Works—and is well respected for her discerning eye for design and her natural artistic ability.

Should you wish to write Pat or Patricia, please forward your letters to Sterling Publishing Company.

CHARLES NURNBERG
STERLING PUBLISHING COMPANY

Current Books by Patrick Spielman

Alphabets and Designs for Wood Signs. 50 alphabet patterns, plans for many decorative designs, the latest on hand carving, routing, cutouts, and sandblasting. Pricing data. Photo gallery (4 pages in color) of wood signs by professionals from across the U.S. Over 200 illustrations. 128 pages.

Carving Large Birds. Spielman and renowned woodcarver Bill Dehos show how to carve a fascinating array of large birds. All of the tools and basic techniques that are used are discussed in depth, and hundreds of photos, illustrations, and patterns are provided for carving graceful swans, majestic eagles, comical-looking penguins, a variety of owls, and scores of other birds. Oversized. 16 pages in full color. 192 pages.

Carving Wild Animals: Life-Size Wood Figures. Spielman and renowned woodcarver Bill Dehos show how to carve more

than 20 magnificent creatures of the North American wild. A cougar, black bear, prairie dog, squirrel, raccoon, and fox are some of the life-size animals included. Step-by-step, photo-filled instructions and multiple-view patterns, plus tips on the use of tools, wood selection, finishing, and polishing help you bring each animal to life. Oversized. Over 300 photos; 16 pages in full color. 240 pages.

Gluing & Clamping. A thorough, up-to-date examination of one of the most critical steps in woodworking. Spielman explores the features of every type of glue—from traditional animal-hide glues to the newest epoxies—the clamps and tools needed, the bonding properties of different wood species, safety tips, and all techniques from edge-to-edge and end-to-end gluing to applying plastic laminates. Also included is a glossary of terms. Over 500 illustrations. 256 pages.

Making Country-Rustic Furniture. Hundreds of photos, patterns, and detailed scaled drawings reveal construction methods, woodworking techniques, and Spielman's professional secrets for making indoor and outdoor furniture in the distinctly attractive Country-Rustic style. Covered are all aspects of furniture making from choosing the best wood for the job to texturing smooth boards. Among the dozens of projects are mailboxes, cabinets, shelves, coffee tables, weather vanes, doors, panelling, plant stands and many other durable and economical pieces. 400 illustrations. 4 pages in full color. 164 pages.

Making Wood Decoys. A clear step-by-step approach to the basics of decoy carving. This book is abundantly illustrated with closeup photos for designing, selecting, and obtaining woods; tools; feather detailing; painting; and finishing of decorative and working decoys. Six different professional decoy artists are featured. Photo gallery (4 pages in full color) along with numerous detailed plans for various popular decoys. 160 pages.

Making Wood Signs. Designing, selecting woods and tools, and every process through finishing are clearly covered. Hand-carved, power-carved, routed, and sandblasted processes in small to huge signs are presented. Foolproof guides for professional letters and ornaments. Hundreds of photos (4 pages in full color). Lists sources for supplies and special tooling. 144 pages.

Realistic Decoys. Spielman and master carver Keith Bridenhagen reveal their successful techniques for carving, feather-texturing, painting, and finishing wood decoys. Details that you can't find elsewhere—anatomy, attitudes, markings, and the easy step-by-step approach to perfect delicate procedures—make this book invaluable. Includes listings for contests, shows, and sources of tools and supplies. 274 closeup photos, 28 in color. 224 pages.

Router Handbook. With nearly 600 illustrations of every conceivable bit, attachment, jig, and fixture, plus every possible operation, this definitive guide has revolutionized router applications. It begins with safety and maintenance tips, then forges ahead into all aspects of dovetailing, free-handing, advanced duplication, and more. Details for over 50 projects are included. 224 pages.

Router Jigs & Techniques. A practical encyclopedia of information, covering the latest equipment to use with your router, it describes all the newest of commercial routing machines, along with jigs, bits, and other aids and devices. The book not only provides invaluable tips on how to determine the router and bits best suited to your needs, but tells you how to get the most out of your equipment once it is bought. Over 800 photos and illustrations. 384 pages.

Scroll Saw Handbook. This companion volume to *Scroll Saw Pattern Book* covers the essentials of this versatile tool, including the basics (how scroll saws work, blades to use, etc.) and the advantages and disadvantages of the general types and specific brand-name models available on the market. All cutting techniques are detailed, including compound and bevel sawing, making inlays, reliefs, and recesses, cutting metals and other non-woods, and marquetry. There's even a section on transferring patterns to wood! Over 500 illustrations. 256 pages.

Scroll Saw Pattern Book. This companion book to *Scroll Saw Handbook* contains over 450 workable patterns for making wall plaques, refrigerator magnets, candle holders, pegboards, jewelry, ornaments, shelves, brackets, picture frames, signboards, and many more projects. Beginners and experienced scroll saw users alike will find something to intrigue and challenge them. 256 pages.

Scroll Saw Puzzle Patterns. 80 full-size patterns for jigsaw puzzles, standup puzzles and inlay puzzles. With meticulous attention to detail, Spielman provides instruction and step-by-step photos, along with tips on tools and wood selections, for making standup puzzles in the shape of dinosaurs, camels, hippopotamuses, alligators—even a family of elephants! Inlay puzzle patterns include basic shapes, numbers, an accurate piece-together map of the United States and a host of other colorful educational and enjoyable games for children. 8 pages of color. 256 pages.

Working Green Wood with PEG. Covers every process for making beautiful, inexpensive projects from green wood without cracking, splitting, or warping. Hundreds of clear photos and drawings show every step from obtaining the raw wood through shaping, treating, and finishing your PEG-treated projects. 175 unusual project ideas. Lists supply sources. 160 pages.

Index

adhesives, 36, 62, 65
Air balloon, 181, 184–185
  alphabet for personalizing, 186
Alligator, 86
Alphabet, 196–199
  with boat pattern, 201–204
  for personalizing puzzles, 186
aniline stains, 240
Apple, 110, 112–113
  rainbow, 130–131

backing materials, 61–62
Baltic birch plywood, 19, 20, 21, 25
band saw, 68
Bear, 88, 89, 136–137
Bear family, 180, 182–183
blades, saw, 38, 39, 40, 46
blade-threading holes, 49, 50
Butterfly, 164–165

Camel, 75, 77
carbon paper, 34
Clown face, 148–149
corners, rounding of, 24–25, 27, 41, 50, 52, 58
Cow, 94, 95
cutting
  around design, 57
  of interlocking pieces, 63–67

Danish oil, 233
decals, 25, 27, 30, 56–57
designing wood puzzles, 23–33
Dinosaur(s), 69–74, 132–133
Disc stand-up puzzle, 220, 222

double-sided puzzle pieces, 23
Douglas fir plywood, 18–19
Dove, 172–175
dowel knobs, 55
Dowel stand-up puzzle, 220–221
Dremel saw, 35, 37, 39, 66
  blades, 39, 40
  for inside openings or piercing cuts, 46
  pin blade, 47
Duck, 98–99, 105
  Puddle, 152–153

Elephant(s), 8, 91–93
  tricky, 178–179
epoxy adhesive, 55
Excalibur II scroll saw, 37

finishing, 53, 230–248
finishing tools, 232
Fish, 160–161
flap wheel sanders, 54
frame puzzles. See inlay puzzles
Fruit, 155, 158–159
frustration, puzzle designing and, 23–24, 26

Giraffe, 86, 87
glue joint, 44–45
gluing
  of dowels, 55
  of puzzle frame, 43–44
  of stock, 15
grain of wood, 35

hardboard, 17–18
hardwood plywood, 19, 20

254

Heart, rainbow, 128–129
Hedgehog, 84–85
Hegner's Multimax-2 saw, 37
Hen, 94, 95
Hippo, 81, 83
history of jigsaw puzzles, 6–7

identifying your work, 248
Indian, 110, 114–117
inlay puzzles, 9, 53–54. *See also* specific puzzle
    patterns making, 119–217
insert puzzles. *See* inlay puzzles

jigsaw puzzles. *See also* specific puzzle patterns
    making, 61–67
Juggling clown, 187–189

Lamb, 88, 90
laun-faced plywood, 20
Lion, 75, 76
lumber. *See also* specific type of lumber
    solid, 14–16

materials, for inlay puzzles, 119
metric equivalency chart, 249
Monkey face, 150–151
Mouse, 78, 79

Name and phone number, 200
natural oil finish, 232
nontoxic coatings, 231
novel and tricky ideas, 218–229
Number puzzle, 190, 192–193
    of stacking blocks, 191, 194–195

Owl, 166–167

paints, latex and acrylic, 234–236
patterns
    removal from sawn pieces, 36
    reproduction of, 35
    transferral of, 34
Pear, 110, 111
personalization of puzzle, 25
Photo Mount, 36, 62
Pig, 94, 97, 210–217
plastic puzzle, 223–224
Playful pup, 100–101
plywood, 18–22
Postage stamp, 218–219
pressure-sensitive adhesive backing, 27–28, 29
Puddle duck, 152–153
Puppy, 100–101

Rabbit, 102–104
Raggy Ann, 138–139
    painting and finishing, 241–247
Rainbow apple, 130–131
Rainbow heart, 128–129
Reidle scroll saw, 37–38, 48, 49

Rhino, 81, 82
Robot, 140–141

sanding, 50–54, 238
saw kerf, 42
scroll saw, 35, 37
    Reidle, 37–38, 48, 49
Seal(s)
    with ball, 105, 108
    trio of, 162–163
Shapes, 142–147
Sheep, 88, 90
sheet material, 16–22
slivering, 19
Small whale, 124–127
Snail, 78, 170–171
Snowman, 80–81
softwood, 13, 14
softwood plywood, 18–20
splintering, 18, 50
spray adhesives, 36, 65
Spray Mount, 36
square puzzle patterns, 226–229
Squirrel, 109
stack-cutting, 11, 58–60, 210–213
Stacking blocks, 120–121
    with numbers, 191, 194–195
stand-up puzzles, 23, 28, 118, 220–222
    making, 68–118
stencils, 28
stickers, 27–28, 30, 31, 52, 53, 54

templates, 25
thickness of puzzle, 15
Tiger, 75, 76
Train engine, 105–107
tray puzzles. *See* inlay puzzles
Tree, 80
Tricky elephants, 178–179
Trio of seals, 162–163
Tulips, 122–123
Turtle, 88, 168–169

United States map, 205–209

varnishes, 233–234
Vegetables, 154, 156–157

walnut puzzle, 224–225
Watco Danish oil, 233
Whale, 172, 173, 176–177
    small, 124–127
white graphite paper, 34
woodburning tool, 231
wood dyes, 240
wood dyes and stains, nontoxic, 237
wood fillers, 237
wood materials, 13–22
wooly sheep, 88, 90